Forecasts and Faith
Five Keys to Weathering the Storms of Life

DOGWOOD
PRESS

Forecasts and Faith
Five Keys to Weathering
the Storms of Life

To Floyd & Alice —
[signature]
Psalm 9:10

BY
Barbie Bassett

DOGWOOD
PRESS

Library of Congress Control Number
2009942097

Printed in the United States of America

Cover Photograph by Clay Spann

Photograph of Barbie in 2nd grade courtesy of Morehead Photography

Photograph of William, Barbie, and Gracie (Barbie pregnant with baby #2)
courtesy of Pound Photography

Photograph of tornado damage reprinted with permission from
the Madison County Journal @ 2001

Photographs of Barbie with baby Gracie courtesy of Allison Muirhead Photography

Pantene Beautiful Lengths photographs of Barbie Bassett and Stephanie Bell Flynt
courtesy of Greg Campbell Photography, Inc.

Photograph of the Wiggs' 50th anniversary family gathering courtesy of Morehead Photography

Photograph of the Bassett family at the Neshoba County Fair reprinted with permission from
The Neshoba County Democrat @ 2009

Book design by Bill Wilson

First Dogwood Press edition: April 2010
Second Dogwood Press edition: May 2010
Third Dogwood Press edition: December 2010

All scripture quotations in this publication are from the HOLY BIBLE,
NEW INTERNATIONAL VERSION @ NIV @ COPYRIGHT @ 1973, 1978, 1984
by Biblica, Inc. All rights reserved worldwide.

DOGWOOD PRESS
P.O. Box 5958 • Brandon, MS 39047
www.dogwoodpress.com

For my loving husband,
three little blessings, and God-fearing parents

Acknowledgments

This book wouldn't be possible without the unwavering support of my husband, William. My children, Gracie, Will, and Lilly Faith, although small, seemed to understand when I said, "Mommy needs to type on the book," and were so quick to play without me.

To those in my hometown of Marks and in Crowder Baptist Church, the lessons learned in small places can have the biggest impact on a person.

My thanks to WLBT General Manager Dan Modisett and my news director Dennis Smith, not only for believing in me, but for always letting me be who I really am on TV.

Thanks to my publisher, Joe Lee of Dogwood Press, who took a chance on this book—thank you, Joe, for seeing the big picture when it was still in my heart. Thanks to Nancy Baker, my publicist, and to fellow author John M. Floyd, both of whom helped read early drafts.

To my parents, Harold Dean and Brenda Wiggs, who know the meaning of Proverbs 22:6, "Train a child in the way that he should go, and when he is old he will not depart from it." Their sacrifices for me have never failed and continue to this day.

And to my Father, God, thank you for each storm You have allowed to come my way. Each one has increased my faith and strengthened my walk with You. For every storm yet to come, may it have a colorful rainbow filled with spiritual wisdom and revelation for me!

Great Is Thy Faithfulness

Pardon for sin and a peace that endureth

Thine own dear presence to cheer and to guide;

Strength for today and bright hope for tomorrow,

Blessings all mine, with ten thousand beside!

Great is Thy faithfulness!

Great is Thy faithfulness!

Morning by morning new mercies I see.

All I have needed Thy hand hath provided;

Great is Thy faithfulness, Lord, unto me!

Pardon for sin and a peace that endureth

Thine own dear presence to cheer and to guide;

Strength for today and bright hope for tomorrow,

Blessings all mine, with ten thousand beside!

Great Is Thy Faithfulness by Thomas O. Chisholm
(c) 1923. Ren. 1951 Hope Publishing Co., Carol Stream, IL 60188
All rights reserved. Used by permission.

Table of Contents

The First Key

Forecasts and Faith
Five Keys to Weathering the Storms of Life

The First Key: Trust God's Plan for your life.

My story began on May 8, 1972, on a farm in Marks, Mississippi, a tiny Delta town between Clarksdale and Batesville. I had to entertain myself on many occasions, since there wasn't much to do in those parts except work like a dog. As the youngest child of Harold Dean and Brenda Wiggs, I have faint memories of my parents loading me, my sisters Rhonda and Melody, and my brother Doug into the family truck and driving to Crowder (another small Delta town about ten miles away) to chop cotton in the scorching summer sun.

Although I was too young to join in, I was placed on a pallet beneath an overspreading oak to play and wait while I watched the others toil in the heat. It wasn't that I didn't *want* to join in, but I was simply too young. I manned the water jug when I was a little older. My siblings would walk up to the back of the truck and pour the cold water into their plastic cups. I longed for the days when I could be one of the "big kids." After all, if I could chop cotton, it would mean I was old enough to do hard labor, although I never heard my siblings brag about what they did during their summer breaks.

I spent most of my summers tending to my mother's garden. We grew everything we ate and, boy, did I like to eat. I loved sweet potatoes, turnip greens, black-eyed peas, butterbeans, and, above all, strawberries. I didn't appreciate why it was so important to work in the garden, but we didn't have much money to buy groceries elsewhere. The garden provided for the

Me at nine months old

six of us, and Momma wanted me to understand I had a vested interest in making sure it grew.

Daddy spent his days working as a postal carrier in town. He would leave early in the morning so he could get home with plenty of daylight left. When he arrived around three o'clock each afternoon, he quickly changed into his work clothes and headed back outside to farm the land. It never made sense to me why Daddy worked two jobs. Those are things you just don't understand when you're a child.

We kids would load into Momma's Impala each day and go to school. There was actually just one year when all four of us were in school at the same time: me in kindergarten, and my brother—the oldest—a senior in high school, with my sisters in between. My mother taught at Delta Academy, which was convenient because we could go to school together and come home together. I remember discovering her paycheck one day on the counter. Six hundred dollars for the month. Was Momma rich or what? I kept the finding to myself and walked with my head held high, for I just *knew* my mother was one wealthy woman.

I soon learned better, though, because Momma also had an afternoon ritual. She would change into her work clothes, just like Daddy, and go outside to pick the garden. She expected me to help, too. I would be all tuckered out from a hard day of learning and Momma wanted me to work even more. She often told me how important it was for us to learn how to grow food and know how to work, and Daddy said many times that hard work never killed anyone. Those words taught me some valuable life lessons and rang over and over in my head for years to come.

***

Playing in the backyard and staring at the sky, I used my imagination to make animal shapes out of the puffy clouds. I would lie on the ground, closely studying one cloud. A minute would go by, and the same cloud would morph into a different animal, right there before my eyes. My imagination would run wild during those days. *There has to be something more to this,* I would think. How are those big puffs of white globs able to do that? I would have to find out more.

The weather always fascinated me as I grew up. In the flat Mississippi Delta, you could see tornadoes from miles away. Or in our case in the dry summers, we would watch dust devils dance in the soybean fields. Storms would form quickly and blow Momma's ferns in the wind. Every few years we even woke to discover a blanket of snow on the ground. It wouldn't last long, but it was sure to get us a day off from school.

So I realized at an early age the importance of weather to my life on the farm. Good crop harvests usually equaled a few new clothes, which we bought in Clarksdale or Batesville. Bad farming seasons meant no new clothes and no vacations. If you've ever been part of a farming family, you know there are more bad years than good. The weather controlled the economy in our home.

I often wondered if my classmates knew my clothes were homemade. What would they say if they knew? I was the only one I knew of in my class whose family income was seasonal—Daddy kept the post office job for us to have an income during those months when there were no crops to harvest or during those rainy seasons when he lost everything he'd just planted due to

The Wiggs Family in 1977: Harold Dean,
Brenda, Doug, Rhonda, Melody, and me

the flooding rains. I always felt a little different because of my clothes, but my mother made it sound like something special. Just think, she told me, no one will have the same clothes you have. And she was right. While some of my friends would often see their outfits on someone else walking down the street (after loaning them to friends), I never had to worry about that. We didn't get a discount at school because my mother taught there, but her paycheck helped with some of our bills as well as extracurricular activities like piano lessons and 4-H.

We spent lots of time at Crowder Baptist Church. Daddy was a deacon and taught Sunday school. Momma was a WMU (Woman's Missionary Union) director, and she taught Sunday school as well as serving on several committees. We walked through the doors every Sunday morning and Sunday night, and Wednesday night for prayer meeting. If we had activities that interfered with church, we didn't do them. It was that simple. For my parents believed church would reinforce what they were teaching us at home and vice versa. I never complained about the unwritten family rule because my closest friends had parents who believed the same way.

When I became a teenager and going out on Saturday nights became part of my social life, it was harder and harder to get up on Sunday mornings for church. "If going out on Saturday night is going to make you so tired you can't get up and get to church on time on Sunday mornings, this cattin' around on weekends is going to stop," Daddy said. Needless to say, I quickly learned how to jump out of bed when he called the first time on Sunday mornings so my Saturday night privilege wasn't taken away.

But after attending GAs (Girls in Action) one Wednesday night, I learned of people living in other countries all around the globe who made it their profession to be missionaries. I found it fascinating that these ordinary people would leave the comforts of home and travel to a foreign land to tell others about Jesus. I liked the "telling" part of the Great Commission in the Bible, but I cringed at the thought of the "going" part. Being the baby of the family, leaving Momma and Daddy was the last thing I wanted to do.

So I had to break the news to my mother at age eight: I felt I was supposed to be a missionary and was none too happy about it! My mother beamed with delight and wanted to know why I wasn't elated with my newfound revelation.

"Because I don't want to go to China," I said. "I don't want to go to Africa. I don't want to go to Brazil."

In a way only a mother can explain to her child, though, Momma took me aside and explained how missionaries are people called by God to do a special job only He could call them to. She said there were missionaries all around us: secretaries, lawyers, doctors, mothers, fathers, and teachers. I knew them already—I just didn't see them in a missionary way.

"If you're a Christian," she said, "you're automatically a missionary by default."

But how could I be a weather forecaster and still be a missionary?

You see, I wasn't the cutest thing on the farm. I was very overweight, wore glasses, had braces on my teeth, and had dark, curly hair.

That's me in 2nd grade. Look at the chubby cheeks.

"What do you want to be when you grow up, Barbie?" I would get asked.

"I want to be on television giving the weather," I'd say.

They usually chuckled, rolled their eyes, and walked away. When one man in our town asked me that same question and I gave my answer, he said, "That's it, honey, dream big." Was I really dreaming? Shoot, I just thought that's what I was supposed to do in life. I didn't think I was dreaming it. But when people took one look at me, they apparently didn't see the type of person who they thought would be on television. After all, how many women have you seen doing weather who are overweight, wear glasses, and have braces on their teeth?

Like many other kids, I was called names. Recess at school wasn't fun. That fifteen minutes of the day was torturous.

"Hey, fatty Barbie."

"There's the girl who wants to be on TV. Yeah, right."

Others would tell me that if I were serious about being on TV, I'd have to lose weight. As I would put on my school clothes and look in the mirror, I'd think maybe they were right. *Maybe I'm not cut out to do this.* The bigger I got on the outside, the smaller I felt on the inside.

***

Each morning before school, Momma would slice apples or peel oranges for me to take in my lunch box for recess. I began to notice that my snacks were disappearing from my lunchbox. I would quietly ask my teacher if I could walk down the hall to speak to my mother—remember, she taught there—and most of the time they would oblige. She figured out before I did that someone was stealing my recess snacks. But just like any mother would do, she would open up her desk drawer and pull a plastic sandwich baggie out of her purse with sliced apples or a banana. My mother was giving up her own snack so I could have one.

I would sit quietly in the car with Momma as she drove us home.

"How was your day?" she would ask.

"Not too good. I was called 'Chubby Cheeks' today."

My mother would look at me with all sincerity and say, "It doesn't matter what you look like on the outside. What counts is on the inside. You let God work on the inside, and He'll take care of changing the outside, all in His time."

My parents were so supportive of me. I honestly believe if I had told them I wanted to be the first female astronaut to land on the moon, my daddy would have said, "I know you will!" There wasn't anything I could dream that was too big for me, according to Daddy. "But you're going to have to get a good education," he told me. "There aren't that many girls on television doing the weather, if that's what you want to do. You need that education."

Daddy told me people might take away my possessions, but they could never take away my knowledge.

***

As I grew older, the weight just didn't come off the way it did for other girls I knew. I'd been told that when people get taller, the chubby look (whatever that is) miraculously goes away. Mine didn't. Momma decided to take me to the doctor and find out why I was gaining weight instead of losing it. Our physician did a few blood tests and asked a series of questions: are you tired, do you have energy throughout the day, are you eating less but still gaining weight? The results came back: I had hypothyroidism.

Generally speaking, my metabolism didn't work as well as that of other kids. This made me tired a lot of the time, left me with low energy, and meant I had to work harder in order to lose weight. He sent me home with a synthetic thyroid medication, which would give me the boost my thyroid needed.

After watching a beauty pageant on television one night, I was enamored with the shiny, glitzy gowns the girls wore. Their hair was big and teased and heavily sprayed, their makeup perfect. That's the way I wanted to look. But one glance in the mirror would tell me I wasn't meant to be on anybody's stage.

When I was in the ninth grade, though, an announcement was made over the school intercom about the upcoming beauty review pageant. On the way home from school that day, I asked Momma if I could enter the competition. I promised to do my best at losing weight and getting fit.

After school every afternoon, I put on my shorts and work shirt and walked the long gravel road that ran alongside our house. After sweating for thirty minutes or so, I would go in my room, close the door, and do some pushups and lunges. I experimented on weekends with makeup. If I saw a celebrity on a magazine cover, I would pick up the cover and examine how her makeup was done. Once again, I would stare at myself in the mirror. I would try to copy how each lash was meticulously separated, and to find the perfect pucker color for the lips.

Taming the curly hair was next. In the same way, I would look at the latest styles and try to work that same magic on my own tresses with hot rollers, sponge rollers, and curling irons. Some days I looked as if I'd had a run-in with an iron because my forehead and neck were red with burn marks from styling my hair.

***

A month went by. I was having success with my weight loss, and it was time to find a dress. Momma was convinced she could make the dress of my dreams, so we drove to the fabric store in Batesville to look at patterns and material. But I didn't find the perfect dress. "Here's an idea," the lady at the counter said. "Let's pick and choose what we like from various patterns. That way, you can have an original dress." What an idea. Mom was up to the challenge, and I had every bit of confidence in her seamstress ability.

So we picked out a navy blue sequined bodice that went nicely with a navy blue taffeta material for the skirt. We picked bugle beads, which we would have to string together in order to make capped sleeves. Then we adorned the bodice with rhinestones.

Momma worked for hours on the Original Pageant Gown. While she sewed, my piano teacher, Martha Lee Hinton, offered to teach me how to walk properly. Several minutes of our weekly piano lessons were spent with me pouring out my heart on how inadequate I felt. "Let me tell you something you may not know," Mrs. Hinton said. "I was Miss Delta State University back in the 1960s. If you want to learn how to walk on stage, I'll teach you everything you need to know." For several days leading up to the beauty review night, Mrs. Hinton taught me how to turn, smile at the judges, and glide across the stage, all while exuding confidence.

When the big night came, I learned I was the only ninth-grader signed up for the pageant! That meant I would be competing against high school girls. I overheard someone in the dressing room mutter, "You know you won't place." I just tried

*I won the title of "Most Beautiful" my senior year at Delta Academy.
That's Will Cassidy, who was "Most Handsome."*

to get that out of my head and think about all the encouragement from my parents, Mrs. Hinton, and others who were rooting for me.

***

Just as Mrs. Hinton had instructed me to do, I walked across the stage slowly and with each turn of my head, I stared the judges down with the best smile I could muster. I felt the spotlights make my dress sparkle. *Even if I don't place,* I thought, *I'm totally okay with the outcome. I've done well.* There I stood with the older girls on stage for the final lineup. The ballots had been turned in, and all that was left to do was announce the top five.

The emcee said, "And the fourth runner-up tonight is contestant number 17, Barbie Wiggs!" I was elated and really didn't hear much else that night. Over the years, I would go on to place in the Top Five every year and won the title of Most Beautiful my senior year at Delta Academy. Not bad, I thought, for a girl who had been teased so much just a few years earlier.

After graduating from high school, I packed my bags for Mississippi College and headed to Clinton. I was randomly placed with a roommate from Clinton, a girl named Missy Elkins. She knew the area well and said if there was anything I needed, she knew where to find it. One afternoon she asked if I wanted to go to the bank with her. She needed to withdraw some money, and we pulled into the drive-thru at her bank. She pulled something from her purse that resembled a credit card. She slipped the card into a machine, typed in a number, and voila— money came pouring out! I had never seen such a thing, and my eyes were wide open with amazement. When we got back to the dorm room that afternoon, I called my parents collect to tell them what I had just witnessed.

"Then Missy put a credit-card-looking thing in the machine, and money just came out of nowhere!" I told them. They could tell I was excited. I later heard the contraption referred to as an ATM.

As you probably figured out, we didn't have those in Marks.

***

I got involved in everything I could at Mississippi College. I tried out for several plays, musicals, and even entered the Miss Mississippi College pageant. I made the Baptist Student Union's drama troupe, which traveled the state witnessing through drama. I even joined the forensics team. I did anything I could do to help me get over my fear of being in front of people and being called names. The more extemporaneous the job, I figured, the better.

There was no meteorology program at Mississippi College, so I decided to major in Mass Communications. This would teach me the basics of how to tell a story: a weather story, or so I called it. Not only did I learn the basics of being behind the camera, but I also learned what it took to be in front of the camera. I met with the head of the Communication department, Dr. Billy Lytal, and told him I felt I was being called into television meteorology.

"You can do this, Barbie," Dr. Lytal said. "We've never had someone from MC go that route, but if anybody can, I believe that person to be you." Hearing Dr. Lytal's confidence in me was a plus.

I went every fall, spring, and summer, and graduated from college in three years. With graduation behind me, there was only one thing to do: head to Mississippi State University in Starkville and work on a Master's degree with an emphasis on broadcast meteorology.

***

During those two years at MSU, though, I felt so lost. Most of my classmates had undergraduate degrees in physics or math. Those guys could spit formulas in their sleep. My undergraduate degree concentrated mostly on getting a product on the air for television or radio. I sat through many of the classes with my eyes glazed over and hearing the professor sound like the classroom teacher in the Peanuts cartoons: "Wah, wah, wah, wah, wah…"

But why would I have felt the tug on my heart from God to go to MSU and continue in broadcast meteorology if it weren't

His will for my life? Was I wasting my time and my parents' money? I began to second-guess myself. *There's just no way I can ever be as smart as these guys*, I thought. I was way out of my league, and I was also the only female in the broadcast meteorology program.

My classmates, though, invited to me to a Starkville hangout one afternoon after a test. So I tagged along and tried my best to fit in with the guys. After *they* had a few drinks—I wasn't drinking—they became very opinionated as we talked about our dream jobs in the television weather industry.

"I just hope I can make it through the semester," I said.

"Oh, please," one guy said while holding a beer. "You'll get hired before any of us because you have boobs."

The table broke out in laughter. I stiffened up and said, "No, my daddy said I just needed to get a good education." One of the guys leaned over and mockingly said, "Your *daddy* doesn't know what he's talkin' about."

This made my heart sink. Was it possible I would be hired just because I was a woman—not because I was a qualified meteorologist? Surely, my employers would be impressed with my degrees and not with my female assets…wouldn't they? I remembered what Momma said: "It doesn't matter what you look like on the outside. It's the inside that counts."

I kept her words tucked in my brain and pressed on.

***

I persevered and continued to pray. *Lord, if I'm supposed to do this, You're going to have to help me!* I kept feeling the nudge to stay the course, although at times I wanted to quit, go home, and admit I'd made a bad career choice. I dug deeper in the quiet time I had with the Lord and prayed earnestly for answers. I also made my broadcast debut, interning for three months on WCBI-4, the CBS affiliate in Columbus.

In May 1995, Dr. Mark Binkley, the director of the broadcast meteorology program at MSU, posted job openings on the bulletin board of the student lounge. He encouraged those of us who would be graduating soon to apply for any and every opening. He made resumé tapes of the graduating students who were eligible for job openings and sent them to interested news directors. That spring he had nine candidates: eight males and me. My tape caught someone's eye in Chattanooga, Tennessee, and I received a phone call from Jim Church, the news director at WTVC-9, the city's ABC affiliate. He had an opening for a weekend meteorologist and wanted me to interview for it. After all the fear and insecurity that accompanied me during those two years in Starkville, suddenly I had a shot at a meteorology job right out of school.

Momma rode with me as we drove the five hours to Chattanooga. I interviewed for the job, did an on-camera audition, and was offered the job the next day. But graduation was just around the corner and I was so close to having the meteorological knowledge I needed in order to be taken seriously in a male-dominated profession. I sure couldn't leave school before the semester was over and not have a degree.

"You'll work for us on the weekends and travel back and forth to Starkville until you finish your schooling," Jim Church told me. "We'll pick up the tab for your hotel and food until you graduate and move here."

And just like that, my television weather career was about to take off!

***

My last months in graduate school were very busy. Not only was I working weekends and struggling to keep my head above water academically, I was also volunteering with the Mississippi Hugh O'Brian Youth Leadership program (HOBY). Watching my parents while I was growing up, I noticed they always found time to be involved in events and activities that benefitted others. It wasn't uncommon for my mother to spend hours making food for someone who was sick or had just lost a loved one. If Daddy saw someone broken down on the side of the road, he would immediately pull in behind them and offer assistance. My parents didn't know it, but they were teaching me the importance of serving others.

I agreed to be the HOBY chairperson for the state of Mississippi in 1995. This put me in charge of teaching over 200 high school sophomores the characteristics of leadership, service, and volunteerism. The annual HOBY weekend seminar was at Millsaps College in Jackson. My committee and I had planned all year and were determined for it to be successful. I asked Jim Church if I could be off Memorial Day weekend to fulfill my obligation. He very kindly gave me permission.

Never in a million years did I think I would meet my future husband there.

The first picture taken of William and me after we met at the HOBY conference in 1995

***

William Bassett was a single, handsome paramedic supervisor who worked overnight shifts. Like the rest of the HOBY counselors that weekend, he wanted to help teenagers learn to make good choices for their future and find their niche in the world.

I immediately spotted William in the crowded room of counselors during orientation before the students arrived and introduced myself. I spent the weekend making sure the leadership training went smoothly, which was my primary responsibility. I also tried to figure out how I could get to know William better.

We sat and talked during every free moment. I learned where he was raised and about the values he had. I was instantly smitten. There was only one problem: I was moving to Tennessee. On the last day of HOBY, we said our goodbyes, and he promised to call me. And he was good to his word. The next day, I received a phone call from William. We began a long-distance dating relationship. He was living in Jackson, and I was headed to Chattanooga.

Although I was excited about this new part of my life and was working in a field I loved and in which I felt more and more confident, I wondered if God had abandoned me—did I have what it took to survive away from home? Excited but nervous, I moved to Chattanooga and settled into a one-bedroom loft apartment at the foot of Signal Mountain. I was now in a big city and knew no one, except my television co-workers. I had truly grown up and left home for the first time, and the man I was falling head over heels for was hours away. How could this relationship survive?

***

My new job was comprised of general-assignment reporting three days a week, with weather on the weekends. I had a lot to learn. The first day involved oodles of paperwork to make me a full-time employee, including my signature on a two-year contract. After the paperwork was completed, I was sent to a photographer who took a series of professional head shots—my first publicity photos. I enjoyed my first day feeling like a celebrity, although there wasn't the first person there who knew, or cared, who I was.

"I don't like your last name," Jim Church told me in his office. "Barbie Wiggs sounds like Barbie Weeks or Barbie Wicks. We could change it to Barbara something, maybe. What's your middle name?"

"Carol," I said.

"That's it. How about Barbara Carol? But we'll need to change the spelling of Carol so it looks like a last name and not a middle name."

I actually liked the idea of being called Barbie Carol.

When Momma got mad at me as I was growing up, she'd call out "*Barbie Carol*" at the top of her lungs, and I'd come running. I didn't like the idea of using Barbara on the air, though.

"Well, my name isn't Barbara. And, I'm afraid, if someone were to call me Barbara in public, I wouldn't respond," I said. So we agreed my new name would be Barbie Carrol.

***

I didn't have an office, much less a desk I could call my

In front of the newsdesk at WTVC-9 in Chattanooga, TN

own. Since I was only in the newsroom a few days a week, there was no need. That meant I had to share a desk with the other reporters. I was happy to do that. But I had to be ready to give up my spot when it was needed by a more seasoned reporter when breaking news happened.

The first story to which I was sent was a press conference. Anyone who's worked in the media can attest to the fact that news conferences are the most boring bits of news to cover. It usually entails someone standing behind a microphone flanked on each side by a handful of other people with nothing to say. There's no action at all, although I was still excited to be on the case. I rode with my assigned photographer in the news station car. It had the sharp-looking NewsChannel 9 logo plastered on both sides. For a moment I felt as if I were waving to the audience in the school's homecoming parade as people strained their necks to see *who* was riding in the news car.

But that silly notion didn't last long, of course. We pulled up to the location, and the photographer looked at me. "If you're planning on working with me, you're going to carry more equipment than that microphone," he said. Obeying orders, I grabbed the camera tripod, which seemed to weigh thirty pounds, and followed him. I noticed reporters from the other stations shouting questions to the officials. I wondered if I should be doing the same. So I came up with a question and hoped I didn't sound like it was my first day ever covering a news story. And the news conference was over just as fast as it began.

We got back to the station, and it was time to pick the sound bites from the interview that would hopefully make it a compelling story.

"I'll pick out the video," my photographer said. "You just pick out the SOT (sound on tape)." After doing what he said, I went back to the computer and started typing something for the anchors to read. It was standard operating procedure for the producers of the newscasts to approve the story scripts. In other words, the photographer could not begin editing the story until the reporter had written something deemed appropriate by the producer. I told the five o'clock producer my script was ready for him to look over.

"This is absolutely horrible," he said with a frown. "Where did you learn how to write? Look how many *that's* you have in this first paragraph. You can say the same thing in different ways without all those *that's*. Go work on it some more," he said.

So much for thinking I knew what I was doing.

After some rewording, the producer approved my script and the photographer edited it. There was nothing left for me to do. My day was over, and I drove back to my empty apartment.

I fixed myself some baked chicken and rice, and sat down on the floor—I had no furniture yet. I turned on the TV and tuned in to our newscast. Soon the anchor was reading my story. I listened intently to every word she said and followed the video, knowing it was my very first contribution to the station. It lasted about thirty seconds, and then it was gone. All of that work for something that didn't even last a minute. *I didn't know this is what reporting is all about,* I thought. But as I ate my dinner that night, I felt two feet taller after having seen *my* story make it to the airwaves.

***

That weekend was my first on the air as a full-time member of the StormTrack 9 weather team. I felt secure and calm at the station, very comfortable with my daily tasks and routine. Not only did I feel I was an official part of the news team, but I was now a resident of Chattanooga.

I began to learn my way around town. I found a grocery store, opened a checking account, found a church, and even found a high-school track I could walk on at night to stay in shape. The weather in Chattanooga, I noticed, was similar to the weather I remembered while growing up. Chattanooga, though, gets more snow than Marks, Mississippi, and what I knew about Jackson. It would reach 95 degrees in the afternoon, then cool down into the 40s at night in the surrounding mountain air. One inch of snow wouldn't shut down the city, either. Drivers were used to it.

I became friends with Melydia Clewell, our morning news anchor. Melydia was a Southern girl too, and we talked each other's language. Melydia and I shopped together, went to lunch together, and even sunbathed together. She had been in the business longer than I had and knew more about what to expect. While standing in the checkout line at the local grocery store one afternoon, a guy said, "You're that weather girl on Channel 9, aren't you?" I smiled back and told him yes.

"You're much prettier in person than you are on TV," he said as he walked away. *What does that mean?* I wondered. It became commonplace for me to be recognized, though, and I was pleasantly surprised at all the comments. One elderly man stopped me in the produce aisle at Walmart.

"Every time I watch you do the weather, you just glow," he said. "There's something special, something different about you." That made me feel great. Now, the Internet wasn't as widely available during that time so I didn't get emails at the station. I received a handful of letters from fans—and even a few marriage proposals out of the blue. Invitations came from civic clubs asking me to speak at their luncheons about the weather. I never turned one down, as I thought it was a way to hone my speaking skills as well as act as a goodwill ambassador for the station.

On my two days off a week—usually Wednesday and Thursday—William and I would get together. Either I would drive to Jackson to visit him, or he would travel north to visit me. William was from Philadelphia, Mississippi. I didn't know much about that town, but I'd heard of its infamous past. There was only one other thing I knew about Philadelphia: it was the home of the Neshoba County Fair.

In July 1995, William asked me to spend a few days at his family cabin at the fair. I would finally get to meet his parents and spend some time taking in the excitement and tradition of the fair. I'd always heard there were three words that described the Neshoba County Fair: hot, hotter, and hottest. And after spending my summers chopping cotton and soybeans on the farm, the last thing I wanted to do was to spend my vacation sweating. But William promised I would have a blast.

So I drove back to Mississippi after getting off work one night. William met me outside Meridian, and I followed him to the Neshoba County fairgrounds. We were greeted by late-night bands that were still playing past midnight amid the stifling heat. Rows of small lights lined the themed cabins. *This has got to be the coolest place on earth*, I thought. After getting some sleep in the air-conditioned second floor of the cabin, I came downstairs the next morning to meet William's parents, Frank and Sudie Kay

Bassett. We hit it off from the beginning. They asked me any and every kind of question, and I returned the favor.

While sitting on the porch that afternoon, I watched people walk by the fair cabin. Some faces looked familiar. *Perhaps I went to college with them*, I wondered. *Gosh, I know her. I didn't know* she *came to the fair.* I assumed the fair would be one large hick-fest, but I found out quicker than anything that I loved every single minute of meeting new friends, seeing old ones, and getting to spend more time with William.

I watched as children frolicked in the red mud after a rainstorm. I smiled as mothers strolled down the dirt pathways with their babies. One muggy morning, I sat on the wooden benches under the pavilion with a paper fan in my hand and listened as politicians gave their best stump speeches. And I noticed when the sun went down, some fair-goers really partied hard!

I drove home to visit my parents the following weekend. It was roughly an eight-hour drive from Chattanooga. Although it seemed like it took forever, I always enjoyed the scenery from Chattanooga to Nashville. Being a geology buff, I admired the rock formations and landscape of the natural terrain. My parents knew I had struck up quite a friendship with William by then, and Momma knew I'd been traveling a lot more often to Jackson than to their house in the Delta.

"I have a feeling you're going to marry that boy," she said.

"Oh, I know I am," I told her with a big smile. "I'm just waiting for him to decide he can't live without me."

***

Over the next few months I continued to work as a reporter and weekend meteorologist. Being the "low woman" on the totem pole, I worked most holidays and often worked long stretches without a day off while substituting for the chief meteorologist, Neal Pascal—who worked the evening newscasts—and our morning meteorologist. Again, though, I was single and didn't have family obligations at home. I didn't mind the extra hours a bit.

Since William worked the night shift, I would stay up late and wait for his phone call before nodding off to sleep. I had to learn how to cut back my food budget a bit in order to afford my monthly phone bill and gasoline money. By then he and I were talking about the future. It was becoming more and more likely I would spend the rest of my life with him, or at least I wanted to. The days in between visits were so lonely and seemed so long. "Absence makes the heart grow fonder," my mother would say, and she must have known what she was talking about.

At work, I continued to get to know the other reporters. I paid attention to how they wrote their stories and made them relatable to the viewers. I listened to the questions they asked their subjects: who, what, where, when, why, and how. When I wasn't assigned to cover a story in the newsroom, I spent time in the weather lab. I watched how Neal Pascal worked, how he built his weather graphics, how he arrived at his forecasts every afternoon.

I also listened when he spoke to viewers who called with what I thought were the simplest of questions: Why is the sky blue? What causes rain? How hot is it going to be today? Not once did he ever act as if those callers were interrupting his day, and that made an impression on me. I noticed how Neal stood in front of the chroma key wall during his weather presentations and gestured at the maps on the TV monitors in the studio (which the viewers were seeing on their screens at home). I listened carefully as he explained the different meteorological terms and used them in ways viewers would understand. *This is the kind of meteorologist I want to be,* I thought.

I'd heard it said before that the best practice you can get in life is to act like the person you want to be. When I did the weather, I wanted to be the kind of person viewers liked, someone whom they might want to meet for coffee or ask over for lunch or dinner. I had seen other anchors and meteorologists who acted snooty, and a couple of times I'd admired someone on television only to meet him in person and be snubbed by him. "Don't ever act like you're better than anyone else," Daddy told me as a child. And just because I was now on television,

I wasn't about to start.

***

I was happy in Chattanooga after a few months of living there, and I liked working at the TV station. There was only one problem. I was deeply in love with William Bassett. One weekend when he came to visit, we made a trip to a local jewelry store "just to look" at engagement rings. I knew something was going to happen. I just didn't know when.

A couple of weeks went by until our next visit. William came to Chattanooga again, and we'd planned to go out to dinner. We sat down to catch up on each other's week when, all of a sudden, William didn't just drop down on one knee.

He got down on both and asked me to marry him.

He pulled out an internally flawless, emerald-cut diamond ring, and I said *yes* right there! I beamed that night when we had dinner at Olive Garden, and I casually mentioned to the waitress that we had just gotten engaged and flashed my new ring. She congratulated me and brought a surprise to our table after the meal. It was a large piece of chocolate cake, on the house. What a sweet ending to the first night of the rest of my life with this man. The next time I went to Marks to see my parents, William met me there. While my mother and I kept busy in one of the back rooms, William humbly asked Daddy for permission to marry me.

***

Once back in Chattanooga, I shared my good news with my co-workers and church friends. It was such an exciting time. But Jim Church, my news director, was about to change all that, at least temporarily. This was in October 1995.

"So, when are y'all going to get married?" he asked.

"Sometime next year," I told him.

"Is he going to live in Jackson and you live here?"

What a crazy question, I thought. "Why would you think that?"

"Remember," Jim said, "you signed a two-year contract with us."

I quickly realized that getting married was not an acceptable reason to be released from a contract. Every bit of hope I had came crashing from the sky.

***

William and I discussed every "what if" we could. We continued to work at our careers and just pray—pray for guidance. The last thing we wanted to do was to wait another year to get married. Even more so, we refused to get married only to live apart. "It would only be for another year that you'd have to live apart," Jim Church said. But that was not an option, as far as we were concerned.

We decided to get married in May 1996, which would mark the halfway point of my contract with the Chattanooga station. If need be, we decided William would leave his job and move to Tennessee to be with me for my last year. Something just didn't feel right about that, though. After much prayer from both of us, I felt a sense of peace about asking my news director if the station would consider releasing me from my contract.

But before doing so, I received a call one afternoon while working in the weather lab at the station.

"Barbie, this is one of William's dispatchers," a woman said. The tone of her voice really frightened me. "William is on a truck (ambulance) and says he wants to talk to you. I'm going to patch him through," she said. "The next voice you'll hear is his."

"Hey, I just wanted you to know I love you," William said.

"What's going on," I asked. "Why are you calling me?"

At that moment, Jim Church came striding into the weather lab. He said the AP (Associated Press) was reporting a hostage situation in Jackson. With William right there on the phone, I asked if he knew anything about it.

"I'm in the middle of it," William said.

I heard shouts in the background. Then William's voice was muffled.

"Did you hear that? A bullet just flew past my truck!"

By this point I was terrified.

"Gotta go," he said. "We've got someone shot. I'll call

you later. I just had to tell you I love you."

The phone went dead.

Another hour went by before the story unfolded from our news sources: A man parked near an abandoned PoFolks restaurant in Jackson and unloaded his arsenal of weapons and a can of gasoline. He randomly fired his gun and killed a man who had pulled into the parking lot. As the ambulance pulled up to assist the wounded driver, the paramedics were fired upon. One bullet struck a newspaper reporter covering the story from a nearby hotel. Before it came to an end, the man set the restaurant ablaze and committed suicide. William, thankfully, called me that night.

"I just felt like I needed to talk to someone before things got worse," he said.

I was glad he chose me.

***

In March 1996, I asked to have a closed-door meeting with Jim Church, my news director. My legs were shaking and my heart was fluttering. *God, be with me,* I prayed. I sat in his office and was transparent with my boss.

"I love him and can't see myself being happy here if I were to stay on for another year," I said. "I just don't feel like I'm supposed to be here."

He raised his voice several times, and I could tell he was

angry with me. Although I didn't know it at the time, one of the station's star reporters had just resigned the day before. Jim, who was a nice man, was not in the best of moods.

"What kind of person are you to sign a contract and then want to break the deal?" he asked.

"I'm not a bad person, and I'm not one to back down from my word," I told him. "My parents taught me better than that."

He looked me straight in the eye. "Obviously, you weren't listening to them," he said. He told me to leave his office and said he would let me know when he'd made his decision. I left his office and walked to the bathroom. I felt like a whipped puppy and broke down in one of the private stalls. I knew I had to get myself together before anyone knew what was going on. I already had an appointment that night to have my engagement pictures made and I didn't want puffy, all-cried-out eyes.

Now I had to wait to find out whether or not I would be released to go home, get married, and live with my soon-to-be husband.

Or if management had decided I had to stay in Chattanooga.

***

Something else was going on in me spiritually by then. In my quiet time, I began studying the life of Noah.

At the end of Genesis 5 when Noah has his sons, the Bible says he was 500 years old. At that point, God told him to build the ark. When the flood waters came, Noah was 600 years old. Do the math: it took roughly 100 years for Noah to build the ark. Do you think you would've run out of patience? But Noah pressed on.

In Genesis 6 and 7, the Bible says something specific about Noah's diligence. Four times in those two chapters, it states, "Noah did all that the Lord had commanded him." Even though Noah probably got tired of building the ark, putting up with the jeers from the townspeople, and waiting on God to make it rain, he stayed the course. He kept his faith and trusted God— who had him building this gigantic boat for a purpose he didn't completely understand. Instead of Noah throwing up his hands and saying, "You're crazy, God. I'm tired of waiting on You, so I'm going to stop wasting my time and busting my knuckles on this stupid boat," Noah trusted God and didn't question His timing.

Shortly after Noah built the ark, it was time to close the door and start the floating. The Bible says the waters flooded the earth for 150 days (about five months). Can you imagine being in that stinky boat with rowdy animals, reptiles, amphibians, and squawking birds for that long? I'm sure that many times, Noah wondered what he'd gotten himself into. Moreover, Noah probably wondered why *he* was chosen to go through this storm. But just because Noah was being obedient, it doesn't mean he didn't feel abandoned. And it doesn't mean he was always brave.

While Noah and his crowded ark were gliding along, Genesis 8:1 says, "But God remembered Noah." Do you think God was floating on a cloud one day and said, "Oh, my heavens. It's been five months, and I totally forgot about Noah! I better look down and check on him."

No. In the Old Testament, to "remember" means to "pay attention to." This passage emphasized God's decision to take action according to His previous commitment to Noah. The commitment, or covenant, that God made to Noah was to wipe humanity from the face of the earth—except for Noah's family (Genesis 9:1). In other words, when God makes you a promise, He always comes through.

Remember, it was so hard for me not to throw my hands up in utter frustration because I wasn't seeing a light at the end of the tunnel when it came to my two years in graduate school. My insecurity in not feeling equal to my classmates made me wonder if the meteorology career I felt called to pursue would ever take off. Why would God call me into this career field only to have me give up? Yes, I'd been hired in Chattanooga and had made the most of a pretty good situation. But now, I'd picked the worst possible time to meet the man of my dreams and fall in love. They say timing is everything, but it sure wasn't in this case. How would William and I make things work? What would my news director do? Would the station be so mad that I'd be blackballed in the business?

I had so many unanswered questions and felt as though I was dependent upon someone else's timetable and not my own. I began to wonder if I should take control of my own life and *not* wait on God to provide His guidance. But something told me to hang on, that God wasn't finished with me. Sometimes, what we want isn't ready for us exactly when we want it, and we end up getting ourselves in trouble because we refuse to have the patience to wait until God works it out for us. So the next time you think about taking things into your own hands because it isn't working out the way you wanted and you think God is dragging His heels, remember this:

Impatient can easily be turned into *I'm Patient*.

God has allowed a particular storm in your life for reasons only He knows. Just as He was faithful to take care of Noah, He is faithful to you and will see you through.

The First Key: Trust God's plan for your life.

He has a rhyme and a reason. Be obedient to what the Lord is telling you to do and trust His hand, even though your boat may start rocking to and fro. Remember, Noah got to see his rainbow in Genesis 9:13. In the same way, God is going to show you what's on the other side of your storm. But you've got to trust Him in order to make it past the thunder and lightning.

The Second Key

Forecasts and Faith
Five Keys to Weathering the Storms of Life

The Second Key: Praise the Lord, even when things aren't going your way.

Two days after my meeting with Jim Church, I noticed a letter in my mailbox at the TV station. It hadn't been sent through the postal service—there was no stamp—and my name was handwritten on the outside of the envelope. I opened it and read a letter from station management agreeing to release me from the second year of my contract.

In return for a payment of $3,000. My heart sank.

They were offering me a contract buyout. It was the only way they would accept my leaving early to get married. In order for the offer to stand, though, the money, I was told, must be paid in full within two weeks.

I don't have three thousand dollars, I thought. *Where did this number come from?* I just knew there had to be a mistake. But while I was walking to my desk to get my story assignment for the day, Jim walked by.

"Get my letter?" he asked.

"Yes, sir," I said. "I'd like to speak with you about it."

He asked me into his office and closed the door. I sat across his desk and told him how grateful I was that they were agreeing to release me from my contact so I could get married and move back to Jackson. But here I was just starting out, hardly had any money to my name, and didn't see how I could come up with three thousand dollars in two weeks. I felt hot, alligator-sized tears welling up in my eyes and tried to hold them back.

"Listen," he said. "You're young and inexperienced and have a lot to learn. I can accept that. We'll come down to two grand on the buyout, but that's as low as we'll go. I suggest you take it."

The meeting was over. I told him I understood and went straight to the bathroom and cried. Sure, I was thrilled he'd come down a thousand bucks, but two thousand wasn't giving me much room to breathe. I called William and told him what had just happened.

"We can come up with that," he said. "We'll make this work. Thank them, and let's get to planning our future."

I went home that night to find something—anything— of monetary value. *Maybe I can pawn enough jewelry to come up with the money. I have that fur coat I won at Miss Hemisphere. That alone should bring in fifteen hundred! And the ring Momma and Daddy gave me should bring in at least two hundred.* I couldn't believe I was actually considering pawning things with such memories attached to them. But I couldn't imagine what else to do to raise the money.

The following day, I took several rings I'd been given over the years by old boyfriends to a pawn shop. I also brought my silver fox coat. I walked in that place feeling so expensive— never in my wildest dreams did I think I would walk out of there without at least two grand.

"For the rings," the clerk said, "I can give you one-fifty. For the coat, I can spot you two hundred."

"Are you kidding me?"

"Sorry. That's all I can do."

I thanked him for his time, picked up my things, and moped out the door.

I am an admitted saver, a packrat. I come by it naturally. My parents never had credit cards when we were growing up. If they didn't have the money to buy whatever they wanted, they didn't buy it. And I don't remember them ever buying a new car. My parents kept their cars and trucks for a minimum of fifteen years. They drove them until the wheels fell off. "Why should we buy a new car when the one we have runs just fine?" Daddy would say.

***

In my quiet time, I prayed for God to somehow direct me to the money. I wanted to be released from the contract. I wanted that obligation behind me and didn't want to ask my parents for financial help.

I wasn't the most diligent at balancing my checkbook, but that was because I tried not to spend much money. The basics were all I needed: food, gasoline, bills. I didn't always open my bank statement. When the next one arrived, though, I was floored when I noticed my checking balance was just over two thousand dollars. I had totally forgotten about the money because I *wasn't* spending it. But there it was, in my account.

God had provided a way out after all.

The next day, I drove to the bank and asked for a cashier's check to be made out to the television station. I gave it to Jim Church later that day. I was officially released from my contract, but agreed to stay on board until the middle of May. This would keep me employed up until the wedding, and it would also give the station plenty of time to hire my replacement.

***

Momma, by this time, was making my wedding dress. In between trips home for fittings and wedding showers, I feverishly phoned the Jackson television stations. What could be better than getting married and returning from my honeymoon with a meteorology job in the city where my new husband already worked?

The news directors at WLBT, the NBC affiliate, and WJTV, the CBS affiliate, told me they didn't have any weather openings.

But there was good news from WAPT, Jackson's ABC station.

"We're actually going to have an opening in a few weeks," their news director said. "Our morning guy is leaving to take a full-time job with the state of Mississippi. Want to come in and do an on-air audition?"

I grinned from ear to ear when I heard that. I asked a few more questions and discovered the station had the exact same weather graphics system we used in Chattanooga. This wouldn't take much training at all.

I drove to Jackson the following week and met with the news director and the outgoing morning weathercaster to go over logistical issues, things like which door to come in at five o'clock the next morning and how to operate the weather graphics computer. Although it was definitely the same equipment, the on-air graphic images had different names. I had to learn what each one was called and how it was saved on the computer.

I was overflowing with excitement. *If I do a good job on*

the audition, I thought, *maybe they'll really hire me. I'd be a good fit.* I knew the Jackson metropolitan area well. Being from Mississippi, there was no need to memorize counties or learn how to correctly pronounce towns like Kosciusko, Shuqualak, or Noxapater.

I didn't get much rest that night because of the swarms of butterflies in my stomach. I was afraid I would oversleep and not wake up in time to make the drive from William's apartment in Ridgeland to the television studio in west Jackson. I slept with one eye open and fixed on my alarm clock. I hoped my aqua blue suit would jump right out at the camera, and my hair wouldn't drop like a rock in the early-morning Mississippi humidity.

***

I got up at four o'clock and put hot rollers in my hair. I would let them curl my hair while I drove to the station. I decided to wait until I finished my forecast graphics before putting on my makeup.

"Good morning, sunshine," a tall man said as he met me at the station's side door. "I'm Hank Downey. I'm the morning producer, and I want to make sure you have everything you need to do your job."

I immediately liked Hank. He was friendly, down to earth, sincere, and made a wonderful first impression—I knew he was someone I would enjoy working with. He followed me into the studio with a cup of coffee in hand (I never saw him without his cup of coffee).

"I'll leave you alone to do your job," he said. "You call me if you need me. I'm right there in the newsroom," he said as he pointed across the way.

I sat down in the weather office and began my forecasting. I carefully made the graphics I would show in just over an hour. I checked and double-checked everything, even the spelling on my weather graphics—the last thing I wanted to do was make a silly spelling mistake on the air and look like an idiot. I found the clicker that was used to cycle through the on-air graphics and began to rehearse.

"With high pressure over the area right now, folks," I said, "don't expect a chance for rain anytime soon."

The studio door opened, and a handsome man walked through with an outstretched hand.

"Hi, Barbie," he said. "I'm Rick Whitlow. Good to have you on board."

I'd watched Rick's sportscasts on WJTV when I was at Mississippi College, so I was already familiar with him as an anchor talent. We chatted a few minutes and, like Hank Downey, it was clear right away I would enjoy working with him.

At 5:30 it was time to head to the dressing room and

put on my makeup. *Need to make a good impression,* I thought, as I tried to make my face look flawless. Just before the newscast started, Rick asked what I wanted to be called on the air.

"I'll be getting married in a few months," I said. "Go ahead and call me Barbie Bassett so I can get used to it."

Suddenly the news open was rolling and the hot studio lights were blazing. The camera operator cued Rick, and off we went.

"Good morning, everyone," he said. "Glad to see you this Wednesday morning. I'm Rick Whitlow, and we'd like to welcome Barbie Bassett to the news desk today, filling in this morning and hopefully giving us a nice forecast." Once I started bantering back and forth with Rick, I felt I was home. He was just so easy to talk to.

***

The show went perfectly. I followed every move and signal the camera operators gave. I kept a close eye on the newscast rundown, wanting to make sure I didn't get caught off guard or out of place along the way, and the hour-long newscast seemed to end just as quickly as it began.

"Nice job, everybody," came Hank Downey's voice over the intercom. "Let's do it again tomorrow."

Rick told me that Hank always gave the anchors and crew

kudos after the show was over. *Even better,* I thought. *I like being part of a team.*

The news director arrived around 8:30 that morning and came straight to the weather center.

"What a fabulous job," he said. "It was like you'd been here for years."

We talked a few minutes as I told him how neat it was to work with a bunch of nice people who had welcomed me from the moment I walked into the building.

"I'll have something in my office for you before you leave," he said. "So be sure to drop by."

I tapped on his door before leaving for the day. I was in a great mood, feeling good about my on-air audition and looking forward to visiting with William one last time before driving back to my apartment in Chattanooga.

"You have something for me?"

It was a contract. God had come through again.

I was squealing with excitement when I burst through William's door and shared the good news. But my excitement faded at his reaction to the offer.

Yes, WAPT wanted me to anchor their morning newscast five days a week, and that was great. But because the station didn't have a noon newscast—and because reporting duties weren't included—it was a part-time job. I would make approximately half the money I made in Chattanooga. William wasn't happy at all about that.

"If we're going to be able to afford a house, you'll have to make more than that," he said.

William, who later became the operations manager with American Medical Response, was a paramedic supervisor with the company at that point. He was also in his final year of pre-med at Mississippi College. He'd lived just as close to the bone in Ridgeland as I had in Chattanooga, so it was critical that we have two full-time salaries—he was exactly right that we wouldn't be able to afford a house payment on his salary alone.

"But I *really* want this," I said. "Maybe it'll develop into something full-time, once the news director sees how hard I'm willing to work."

"Yeah, but what you hope they do for you later won't help us now."

We had our first argument then. Like that of many couples, it was about money.

***

The WAPT news director called the next day to see what I'd decided. I asked for one more day, and William and I continued to discuss the offer. I still really wanted the job, but we would have to pinch pennies in a big way. It appeared the only way we could make it work was if I took a second job to supplement our income.

What do you want me to do, God?

I called the news director the next day and said yes. I stopped by WAPT to drop off my contract and signed it as Barbie Wiggs, given that it would be another couple of months before my last name would change forever. It became a running joke with close friends as to exactly who I was from week to week: I was still Barbie Carrol on television in Chattanooga, Barbie Bassett on TV in Jackson, and Barbie Wiggs when I went home to the Delta. There were times I had to stop and take a moment to remember which name I was using.

That spring was a blur. I worked seven days a week: two in Jackson doing morning weather at WAPT, and the other five in Chattanooga reporting and doing weekend weather. I also made trips home to Marks so Momma could make adjustments to my wedding gown and wrap up any loose ends before our big day. In the meantime, William and I purchased our first home in a quiet Madison County neighborhood. We spent a few hours on my trips to Jackson moving bits and pieces of his belongings from his apartment to our new home. The builder even posted a sign in the barren dirt of the front yard that read, "Future home of William and Barbie Bassett." We drove by the house several times a day just to see our names together in print.

***

May arrived. It was the month I would turn 24 and get married. The time was drawing nearer to my permanent move back to my home state of Mississippi.

I packed my belongings and the furniture I'd bought while in Tennessee. The Chattanooga friends I'd made in church helped me load the moving truck. Everything had to fit because I didn't have the time—or money—to make another trip back to the city. When the truck rolled away, it was the end of my Chattanooga television career as well as my last time in the city.

After the eleven o'clock news that night (remember, Chattanooga is in the eastern time zone), I said goodbye to my co-workers of one year. I wrote notes of thanks to many, and they did likewise for me—that meant a lot. I put my purse on my shoulder, had my makeup bag on the other arm, and walked out to my car. William cranked up the moving van and backed out of the parking lot. As I drove off, I turned back one last time to look at the brightly-lit NewsChannel 9 logo on the side of the building. We drove through the night and made it to Jackson at five o'clock the next morning.

***

We got a few hours of sleep and began unloading my furniture and clothes into our new home. I playfully ordered

William and a friend of his around the house, telling them where to put this and where to move that. All the while, I was envisioning where to put pictures and decorations. We wanted as much unloaded and in place as possible, because we would be husband and wife when we set foot in the place again after the honeymoon. With that in mind, I assembled my wedding trousseau and drove to Marks to spend my last remaining days as a Wiggs with my parents.

Momma and I wrapped up the final plans and double-checked every detail. One last order of business was to purchase the marriage license. This was a special moment because my mother, as circuit clerk of Quitman County, handled the paper-work herself.

***

The morning of May 25, 1996, came early. I couldn't sleep much the night before as we had a special celebration at the wedding rehearsal and dinner afterwards. And, naturally, I was too excited to sleep, as a bride-to-be should be just before her wedding day. I flipped on the morning news and saw rain in the forecast.

"A cold front is on the way, folks, so keep your umbrella handy today," said the weatherman on the Memphis station. "Some of you may get a brief thunderstorm or two and cool you off from the May heat."

Not us, I hoped. There was a bridesmaid luncheon in my honor in just a few hours, and William and his out-of-town friends and groomsmen were teeing off at the local country club to play eighteen holes before our wedding.

***

As it turned out, I couldn't have asked for a more beautiful day at the outset. The sun was brilliant, and the magnolias were in full bloom. We drove to First Baptist Church in downtown Marks to get ready for early pictures. I had decided to get married at First Baptist of Marks instead of my home church in Crowder because my first cousin was also getting married that day. William and I were getting married at six o'clock, and my cousin's wedding was earlier. I offered to move the location of ours to keep the families, florists, caterers, and guests from having any doubts about who was getting married when and where. It all worked perfectly.

Most of the day was a blur. What seemed to take forever—the planning, the organizing, my move from Chattanooga back to the great state of Mississippi—was suddenly over. It was time for me to become the wife of William Bassett.

One by one, my sisters and bridesmaids walked down the aisle. The church pews were decorated with magnolias. On the altar banisters were billows of white tulle, magnolias, and miniature while lights. Each stained-glass window had a magnolia arrangement with a burning candle set inside. As Mrs. Hinton, the piano teacher from my youth, played "Trumpet Voltaire" on the pipe organ, my daddy looked at me with a tear in his eye.

"Are you ready to do this, monkey?" he asked.

I nodded and made one last request of him: "Don't step on my dress, Daddy."

I walked down the aisle with my guests winking, smiling, and mouthing, "Congratulations," all the way to the front altar. There, I found the man I had prayed for as a little girl. My mind went back to my teenage years....

"When I get older, I want to marry a handsome man," I told my childhood friend Lisa Austin. We attended Crowder Baptist Church together during our "boy crazy" years and were active in the youth group and on the puppet team. We often sat up late at night discussing the men we would most likely marry.

"And I just don't think it'll be anyone from here," I added.

"But he's *got* to be cute," Lisa said.

"Oh, totally cute. Wonder if we'll have any kids?"

I actually had an index card outlining what I wanted Mr. Right to be like. When I was in the eighth grade, I had written in my best handwriting the following qualities:

handsome, humorous, kind, giving, smart, doesn't drink, doesn't smoke, is a Christian.

"Does this guy even exist?" Lisa asked with a puzzled look on her face when I showed her the card.

"I hope so," I told her. "I sure won't give up until I find him."

As I got to the altar, there was the man I had dubbed ten years earlier as Mr. Right. Daddy lifted my veil, gave me away, and the ceremony began. But as the minister began to give the background on the first Biblical marriage, thunder rolled outside. Yes, it was one of those storms the Memphis weathercaster had warned about, and the electricity instantly went out. Mother Nature had picked me out of all the people in the world to get married during a thunderstorm. But as I looked around at those who had looks of sympathy on their faces for me on my storm-drenched wedding day, I noticed we were exchanging our vows by candlelight. Our wedding would be romantic after all.

We put rings on each other's hands and the minister gave William permission to kiss me. The minister said, "I now present to you...Mr. and Mrs. William Bassett!" At that moment the electricity came back on, and Mrs. Hinton played "Joyful, Joyful, We Adore Thee" as we walked hand-in-hand back up the aisle.

After more pictures of the wedding party, we made our way to the reception at the country club where guests greeted us with hugs and words of encouragement. Pictures were taken of us cutting the cakes and throwing the bridal bouquet and the garter. We mingled a few minutes longer before we received word that our limo was coming up the long, gravel road. William and I had an escape plan to get us out of our reception and into the limo without getting interrupted. There was only one person who knew how we would leave.

My mother.

We stopped at Millsaps College after the honeymoon. This is where we'd sneak off to talk while at the HOBY conference in 1995

Since my car was at the reception, most people assumed we would be leaving in it. William had disappeared to go get in the limo as I waited behind. Quietly, I whispered to my mother, "It's time. I'll call you when we get there." We kissed and I was ushered out the back door. I hopped into the back of the limo and the driver pulled us in front of the building.

The black tinted windows rolled down, and William and I waved to our guests. "Come on, everybody, they're leaving!" someone yelled. Each guest was given a white balloon filled with helium. As we waved goodbye to our guests, hundreds of balloons were released into the air. William's close friends, who no doubt had plans to delay our getaway by pelting us with rice, shaving cream, and no telling what else, stood there in bewilderment. We had outsmarted them. We rode all the way to the Peabody Hotel in Memphis to begin our honeymoon.

***

A week later we were back in our new home and settled into a routine. William was at his job as a paramedic supervisor for American Medical Response, and I was forecasting morning weather on television. We weren't making much money, but we were happy together and felt invincible. I loved what I was doing at WAPT. The early-morning schedule fit perfectly into my home life. I made friends with an anchor/reporter named Tiffany Tyler, a svelte, blue-eyed blonde from Louisiana. She taught me how to rollerblade, and I worked with her on loosening that thick Cajun accent. Actually, everyone who worked on the morning newscast became friends of mine, from the technical director to the graphics operator to the camera operators—we were all buddies. When you start your day while the rest of the world is asleep, you share a kindred spirit.

Along the way I met Marshall Ramsey, the editorial cartoonist for *The Clarion-Ledger*. I didn't know it then, but Marshall and I would team up many years later to do community service work together. Because Rick Whitlow, Tiffany Tyler, and I interviewed guests every morning, I met politicians, business owners, fashion experts, medical professionals, and everyday people who were more interested in giving than taking.

William and I would see each other for two, maybe three hours at night before it was time for me to go to bed—I made it a point to do that at nine o'clock every night. We spent those few evening hours catching up on each other's days and planning our future. Although we weren't ready to start a family yet, I wondered how we would manage when we felt called by God to have children. Everyone told us how much they cost, how high-maintenance they were, and how your life would never be the same. For now, we would concentrate on paying the bills and trying to save some money each month. When God was ready for us to have children, He would change our perspectives and turn our fears into positives.

I was enjoying WAPT, but I felt there had to be something more. I felt God wanted me to play a larger role in the community. Trying to be patient, I waited for Him to advise me how to make that happen.

***

As May 1998 wound to a close, my two-year contract with WAPT was up. William was still a paramedic supervisor for AMR. We were several years from his promotion to operations manager. We desperately needed more money in our household if we were going to start a family, which we were now discussing often. At the very end of the month, the man who was by then the WAPT news director let me know I was welcome to sign another contract with them and continue as their morning meteorologist.

For the same money and hours, because it remained a part-time position.

That isn't going to work, God. Now what do I do?

This time there was no argument with my husband. William and I were in solid agreement that I couldn't do it. I asked repeatedly if reporting several days a week—as I had done in Chattanooga—could be added to my duties to create a full-time position. The answer was no. The offer was two more years with the same hours and salary, take it or leave it.

I didn't sign. My contract with them expired, and I was

suddenly unemployed.

I called WLBT news director Dennis Smith, whom I'd contacted two years earlier when William and I had gotten married and I wanted to move to Jackson. He'd caught a few of my weathercasts over the last two years and seemed interested that I was no longer working across town. He told me their week-end weathercaster was about to take vacation and asked if I was interested in freelancing for one weekend. I jumped on the chance to work two days for them and was told later that the phones rang off the hook in the WLBT newsroom with viewers who wanted to know if I was part of their team. I couldn't have felt better about the situation.

Until Monday morning.

***

WAPT filed a temporary restraining order in Hinds County Chancery Court to stop me from working at WLBT because of a non-compete clause in my contract. While I was free to work right away at any Jackson newspaper or radio station— and free to work at any Mississippi television station as an anchor talent *other* than in the Jackson market—I could not work on camera with either WLBT or WJTV for a calendar year.

Was I crushed? Yes. I was 26 then, and a full year off the air seemed like a lifetime. What would happen to my career? Would anyone ever want to hire me again? And in the meantime, how were William and I going to pay the bills, let alone think about starting a family? What on earth was I going to do?

***

When bad weather comes to roost over our heads, praising God just doesn't make sense to most of us. One of my favorite stories in the Bible is of Moses and the Amalekites. In Exodus 17:8, we learn of the battle Moses was facing. The Amalekites came and attacked the Israelites at Rephidim, and Moses said to Joshua, "Choose some of our men and go out to fight the Amalekites. Tomorrow I will stand on top of the hill with the staff of God in my hands." So Joshua fought the Amalekites as Moses had ordered, and Moses, Aaron, and Hur went to the top of the hill. As long as Moses held up his hands, the Israelites were winning, but whenever he lowered his hands, the Amalekites were winning. When Moses' hands grew tired, they took a stone and put it under him and he sat on it. Aaron and Hur held Moses' hands up—one on one side, one on the other— so that his hands remained steady till sunset. So Joshua overcame the Amalekite army with the sword.

I doubt Moses was holding his hands up toward heaven just for the fun of it. Did he have nothing else better to do that day? No, I believe Moses was truly praising God. Because if he'd put his hands down, Joshua and his army would have been shredded to pieces.

The Second Key:
Praise the Lord, even when things aren't going your way.

I believe God listens to every prayer we bring before Him. But I also believe God listens even more when we are praising Him through *our tough times*. That's what my mother meant when she told me that my year off the air was a spiritual battle. You fight spiritual wars in the spirit. God knows we are genuine and sincere if we can keep the focus on Him through it all—instead of keeping the attention on ourselves and our problems. Praising God through all circumstances brings His will into focus.

The Third Key

Forecasts and Faith
Five Keys to Weathering the Storms of Life

The Third Key: Forgiveness is not an option.
It is a command.

My departure from WAPT and the weekend stint at WLBT were splashed all over the *Clarion-Ledger*, as well as discussed on Jackson talk radio. Not to mention, I'm sure, at water coolers all over the Jackson area. That's the way it felt, at least, especially in those first days and weeks I was off the air. Our parents and friends were wonderful in my time of need, but there was little anyone could do to console me. I didn't want to leave the house, let alone go out in public and try to enjoy myself without wondering if everyone who recognized me was talking behind my back. I was frustrated by everything that had happened, and angry that my career had been stopped in its tracks as if someone had grabbed the proverbial power cord and yanked it from the wall.

I felt like a failure.

***

But I sure couldn't sit around and feel sorry for myself. Remember, we were now living off William's salary after budgeting for two incomes.

I'm hurt and angry and confused, God. And I REALLY need your help.

Good things soon began to happen.

A friend called and asked if I would serve on a mock judging panel for a contestant who was preparing to compete in the Miss Mississippi pageant. Of course I would help. I had no job and nothing else to do. I walked in and saw a few people I recognized and said hello. Then a precious woman came bopping up to me wearing a grin from ear to ear.

"Barbie Bassett, I am so glad to meet you," she said as she shook my hand. "I'm Dianne Dyar with the Madison County Chamber of Commerce." We were exchanging pleasantries when she asked the question that everybody, it seemed, asked when they saw me. "Why aren't you on TV any more, my dear?"

As always, I tried to be diplomatic. I also knew to be on my toes—I had to start bringing in money to supplement William's salary—and I admitted to Dianne that I was looking for work while off the air. And as it turned out, the Chamber was getting ready to embark on a capital campaign. Dianne wanted to hire someone who could market the Chamber's plan of action, which included an expensive strategic plan.

You better believe I told her I could do it.

I didn't have a lick of marketing experience...although I'd sure marketed WTVC in Chattanooga for a year and, more importantly, I'd done the same for WAPT in Jackson for two years. I'd always tried to act as an ambassador for both stations whether I was on or off the air. I did a lot of public speaking and met a ton of people.

Why couldn't I learn how to help market the Chamber?

Dianne and I met a week later. She offered me the job on the spot. Not only would I work for the Madison County Chamber of Commerce, but it was absolutely fine with her if I worked 500 other part-time jobs as long as it didn't interfere with what I was doing for her.

It wasn't the same as forecasting the weather, but it was a start.

And it was nice to have someone like Dianne believing in me.

***

Over the next few weeks, I met community leaders, business owners, and politicians while working on behalf of the Chamber. I sat through meetings, learned about business, and honed my marketing skills. I was enjoying the work and made good contacts around the Jackson area. I also joined volunteer groups (having learned from my parents our responsibility to give back) and made more friends. Yes, my meteorology education and training were being wasted—or at least were on hold. But I was learning more about public relations, marketing, and business leadership every day. Ever hopeful that I would return to the airwaves the following summer, I let Dianne know that although I was deeply grateful to her, I didn't plan to work for the Chamber forever.

"Well, it's only a year-long job, anyway," she said. "But until then, how would you feel about soliciting Chamber memberships and trying to land us some new members? I'll pay you commission."

Can do, I thought. Not only was I receiving a salary for the work I was doing with the Chamber's capital campaign, but now I could earn bonus money. Other than selling my share of magazines and pizzas in grade school to raise money for our causes at Delta Academy, I'd never sold anything, and the finer points of closing sales sure weren't taught in the synoptic or thermodynamic meteorology classes I took at MSU. I was up for the challenge, though, and sold ten memberships in the first two weeks and was suddenly making more money than I ever made in television. God was providing for our every need, even if it wasn't the way I'd planned.

And He was just getting started.

***

I'd been off the air for over six months by February 1999. I got a call that month from what was then WTYX radio, wanting to know if I would be interested in filling in while their morning newsreader took a week of vacation. Absolutely, I said. It was (almost) like old times, the way I got up in the wee hours to be at the radio station by five o'clock that week, and I went from there to Canton to work at the Chamber the rest of the day. Before long I was working several days a month for WTYX. It led to the offer of flying in the helicopter they shared with—

After getting over the flying jitters, riding in Skycopter-3 was great fun while reporting traffic for WLBT and WTYX.

you guessed it—WLBT for afternoon traffic reports.

Soon afterward, Dr. Billy Lytal, my professor from Mississippi College who encouraged me to pursue my meteorology dreams while I was an undergrad, called and asked if I would be interested in teaching in the Communication department on an adjunct basis. He wanted me to teach a basic meteorology course, something the college didn't offer. He gave me the task of formulating the curriculum and choosing the textbooks, and he even asked if I wanted to teach in the fall or spring semester. That, too, was my choice.

In addition, Dr. Lytal asked if I would teach a public speaking course as well. I loved my years at Mississippi College and was eager to return to a place that held so many good memories. Instead of looking upon the teaching position as a way to discuss the negative publicity that surrounded me at the time, I looked at it as a chance to mentor 15 to 20 students as they prepared for the future. Be ready, I told them, to implement Plan B if a career crisis showed up on their doorstep.

Once again, God was providing. Money was coming in from the Chamber, from Mississippi College, and from the radio station. My days were long, but things at home were much easier as William and I paid bills and continued to set aside money for when we were ready to start a family. It still wasn't the same as doing on the air what I felt God had wanted me to do all along, but He had helped me take several steps in the right direction. During the toughest of career circumstances, I could see God's hand at work. When you're in the middle of a storm, it's hard to realize the sun is shining just above in the clouds. And it was as if blessings were falling from the sky, just for me. I knew where these blessings were coming from because of my willingness to forgive.

***

I counted down the months to my non-compete freedom. The last time I had spoken to Dennis Smith at WLBT, we had agreed to touch base once the year had passed. Sure enough, he called in August.

"Our morning meteorologist is going on vacation," he said. "I was wondering if you would be interested in working a few days for us."

Would I ever!

I walked down the hallowed halls of WLBT and met the likes of Bert Case, the late Woodie Assaf, Walt Grayson, Maggie Wade, and Howard Ballou. These were people I'd watched during my years as a college student and dreamed of working with one day. To know I was within the same walls as these legends gave me great comfort.

Everywhere I went, people asked me, "Are you with Channel 3 now?" I explained that I was only filling in when they needed a meteorologist, as there was no way to know if anything permanent lay ahead. Dennis called again in September, though, and I worked a few more days on the morning show. I was getting the hang of the station's weather computers and their daily routine.

One morning I was chatting with morning co-anchor Melissa Pace after the newscast.

"Don't tell anyone," she whispered, "but I'm turning in my resignation today."

I felt my insides jump with excitement. This could be my chance at working full-time at WLBT! I listened as Melissa described a job in Birmingham she was taking. I confided in her that I would move heaven and earth to take her place.

"Wait till tomorrow and let me make it official, before you talk to Dennis," she said. "But I think you'd be a perfect fit, since you've been filling in the last month."

***

I wanted to burst into Dennis' office right then, but I did as Melissa asked, of course, and waited a full day before calling him from home. I came right out and said I knew Melissa was leaving, and that I wanted the job.

"I thought you were a meteorologist," Dennis said.

"I am," I said. "But my undergraduate degree is in Mass Communication with an emphasis on anchoring and reporting."

I described the reporting and co-anchoring I did in Chattanooga. "And my Master's is in Broadcast Meteorology. The idea was being able to do both in the event a station had an opening for either one. In other words, Dennis, I can co-anchor the news and report for you. And if you ever need someone to fill in for weather, I'll already be on board."

"Well," he said. "That's what we call *marketability*. When can you come in for an audition?"

I drove to WLBT the next night after the six o'clock news and recorded a mock newscast. The director recorded everything I said and did, including how I interacted with the camera.

Dennis called the next day and offered me the morning co-anchor position.

My career at WLBT had begun.

***

My job at the Madison County Chamber of Commerce came to a close. Dianne Dyar and I said our goodbyes and pledged to stay in touch—what a nice lady. I continued to teach at Mississippi College part time, as well as fly in the helicopter leased by WLBT and WTYX and give the afternoon traffic reports.

But working alongside Wilson Stribling (now WLBT's assistant news director), the now-retired Jack Hobbs, and morning/noon meteorologist Paul Williams had to be the most entertaining job I've ever had. Waking up at two-thirty each morning honestly wasn't as hard as it sounded when you had the fun we did. The laughs, the jokes, and the on-camera antics are what we were known for. People tuned in to get their morning news and weather from us, but many told me that they started their day by relating funny things the four of us had said during the newscasts. Some were intentional, but most were off the cuff. The hurt from being away from on-camera meteorology for a year was fading fast, and I now had a peace beyond anything I could have imagined.

Jack Hobbs, me, Paul Williams, and Wilson Stribling.
We dressed up in our 70s costumes for Halloween 2001.

It was clear I was right where God wanted me to be.

***

We drove to Marks for Thanksgiving in November 2001. It's our family custom to have a reunion the day after Thanksgiving, and it was early Saturday morning that weekend when my mother walked into my childhood bedroom where William and I were sleeping. It was about 5:30 in the morning.

"Barbie, y'all need to wake up," she said. "Sounds like a tornado has hit your neighborhood."

William and I both jumped to our feet, and he grabbed his pager to see if he had any messages. Then he called his office and spoke to a dispatcher who confirmed the tornado. I called WLBT's newsroom next.

"It's true," a producer said. "We don't know the specifics, but we've learned there are two deaths so far, and most of your subdivision has blown away."

***

William and I packed our belongings and raced down I-55 back to Madison. We picked our way to our neighborhood and found police cars swarming the highway. A roadblock was set up at the entrance to our subdivision. Trees, branches, and snapped utility poles lined the highway. The farther we drove, the more scared I became. We didn't know what we would find, but by then we knew our house was still standing—another of

William's dispatchers had confirmed it.

A highway patrol officer asked for proof of identification before letting us through the roadblock. William and I both whipped out our driver's licenses, and he waved us in and told us to drive extremely carefully. The distance to our home from that point is about a quarter mile. But the drive seemed like an eternity. We crept along, looking all around, and saw many of our neighbors outside. Some were crying. Others looked shell-shocked. Their eyes showed signs of utter disbelief and devastation.

My neighborhood was demolished by an F-4 tornado in 2001.

Many of the homes looked as if they had exploded.

Home insulation was strewn all around, as were pieces of shredded paper. People were milling about, trying to pick up anything they could find, whether it was theirs or not. The Salvation Army canteen van was parked on the corner. Farther up the street was the American Red Cross, which had set up a disaster response location and was handing out pamphlets to homeowners.

We rounded the corner and saw the homes of our next-door neighbors. The home directly across the street had a collapsed wall and a fully exposed bedroom. The roof of a home right in front of us had been completely sheared off—the gables and attic contents were hanging from the rafters. Our house looked complete until I saw someone walk through one of the open doors.

It was one of the paramedics who worked with my husband.

"Hope you didn't mind," he said when we reached him. "I came through one of your windows that had blown out."

At least our home was still standing. That was a good sign.

There was glass everywhere, though, and as I walked into the master bedroom I came face to face with a truly frightening sight: a two-by-ten piece of wood had been hurled through our bedroom window and landed on top of our queen-sized mattress.

"One of you wouldn't be standing here today if you'd

been in bed when this happened," the paramedic said.

A chill ran up my spine.

I walked into the bathroom to see what was left of it. Bricks had blown off the side of our house, I saw, and had been thrown through the tempered glass window. The bricks had broken holes all through the wall where my vanity was located. Glass filled the garden tub. I walked past my closet. My clothes had been blown all around. I walked outside and saw debris scattered all over the yard. No telling where it came from, but it wasn't from our home.

William's outdoor grill was gone from the back patio, never to be found. I looked up at the eaves of the roof. Each corner of the roof looked as if it had been lifted and put back down again—but not in a square position. Our house, it occurred to me, almost looked as though it had *exhaled*. I walked back through the house to find other damage, and something caught my eye.

On the nightstand next to my bed was my Bible.

It wasn't even touched. Although the west side of our home had taken the worst beating during the storm and glass was blown all through the house with the busted windows, my Bible didn't even have the first page blown out of place.

My Bible had withstood an F-4 tornado.

It was one of the most amazing things I've ever seen.

***

There was no electricity, but we refused to leave our home by itself in the shape it was in. Law enforcement provided round-the-clock security to keep the onlookers and would-be thieves away from our neighborhood. Black and blue tarps were hung on our roof and on the west side of the house. We cleaned up what we could to prepare for the rebuilding. Thinking I had gotten most of the glass cleaned off the floor and out of the carpets, I discovered minute shards of glass embedded in the bottoms of my feet. Like-wise, my clothes looked perfectly normal on the outside, but wearing them felt like wearing thorn bushes. It took weeks to find all the tiny pieces of glass. I can only imagine the way things must have blown around inside our house that day.

The Salvation Army and the American Red Cross fed us most of our meals for the first several days. Many of our neighbors literally had nothing left. Although we weren't facing as many obstacles as they were, I still felt helpless. I'd never felt as needy in my life. I felt violated by nature. We had to move out of our house and into an apartment for three months while construction crews put the house back together.

One afternoon while doing traffic reports for WTYX several days after the tornado, I asked pilot Coyt Bailey to fly me over the neighborhood. I sat in the crew chair as tears dripped down my cheeks. I saw homes that had been flattened, trees stripped of their leaves, and mailboxes twisted like pretzels. I recognized neighbors who were looking desperately through their belongings. One family, I learned later, was searching for their wedding pictures from thirty years ago. Another neighbor was picking up pieces of her great-grandmother's china that had been neatly packed away in boxes and placed in her attic for storage. There was no more attic and, sadly, only remnants of the antique china.

As I looked down and watched the flurry of activity on the ground, I knew their stories. William and I had given up working on our house and had walked through the subdivision offering to help anyone who looked as dazed as we felt. Seeing the damage on the ground and being aware of the tornado path was an awesome sight for a meteorologist.

It changed forever how I covered severe weather.

No longer would I look at a tornado vortex signature on the radar and get excited. No longer would I look forward to breaking into television programming and talking endlessly about where the tornado was headed. Gone were the days of feeling my heart pound when I saw the twisting image on the radar. Having experienced putting our home back together and watching our friends do the same, forecasting tornadoes became sobering. I took it seriously, only because I had been there before and could officially say "done that."

***

WLBT's morning news was becoming even more popular than before. The ratings grew, and my love for the show did as well. Whenever meteorologist Paul Williams took vacation, I put on my weather hat and did the forecast—I had the best of both worlds. WLBT, based on the places I went and people with whom I spoke, was a household favorite with viewers. Receiving emails and phone messages from viewers was a daily occurrence.

But among the feel-good comments were a few things

Reading over scripts before the WLBT morning news

here and there that, well, let's just say we're all sensitive at times.

One morning I awoke with a horrid case of pinkeye. My eyes were too swollen for me to wear my contact lenses, so I put on my glasses and hoped no one would notice. But this gem, among others, was left on the weather center voicemail.

"Barbie, please don't ever wear those glasses again. They are hideous and you have no business wearing them. Throw them away, for God's sake."

Who woke up on the wrong side of the bed that day, hmm?

"Please don't put your hair behind your ears. Your ears are too big to wear that hair style."

Television anchors are public figures. I understand that, and so do all of my co-workers. I guess there are people out there who feel they're providing sage advice by dialing my voicemail and leaving their comments about my appearance. It happens to other anchors, too. I make a note of the more outrageous ones and share them with my audiences when I speak. The anecdotes are always good for laughs.

***

By the fall of 2002, William and I had been married over six years. I'd like to think we were maturing—time surely was passing by. Our careers had stabilized, and we were paying off the debts we'd accrued during our single years. We both thanked

God every day for our good fortune. And we received another blessing that fall.

We were expecting a baby.

We waited almost three months before telling our families. I had hidden the all-day sickness pretty well from my co-workers, but that changed. I was running to the ladies' restroom and getting sick at every commercial break. Then I'd put on lipstick once more, pop a breath mint in my mouth, and walk back onto the set as though nothing had happened. I broke the news on-air to Wilson, Paul, and Jack when I was almost four months along. They were pleasantly surprised and couldn't believe I was able to keep such a secret for so long. I was inundated with emails, letters, and phone calls of encouragement and congratulations from viewers—all of which made me feel good.

My first pregnancy went very smoothly. Other than the nausea continuing after the first trimester, I felt good, big belly and all. In one of my quiet times, I asked the Lord to direct me to a scripture passage I could pray and claim for the new life growing inside of me. The Holy Spirit guided me to Colossians 1:9-10.

"Since the day we heard about you, we have not stopped praying for you and asking God to fill you with the knowledge of His will through all spiritual wisdom and understanding. And we pray this in order that you may live a life worthy of the Lord and

Having fun with Gracie

Singing "Amazing Grace" to Gracie

may please Him in every way: bearing fruit in every good work, growing in the knowledge of God."

That verse was my prayer for our child.

***

My OB-GYN, Dr. Meredith Travelstead, guided me through those last few weeks of pregnancy. And on July 1, 2003, after three pushes, Ashley Grace Bassett was born. We gave her the middle name Grace after one of my favorite songs, "Amazing Grace." We would call her Gracie for short. Dr. Travelstead gave me one warning after the short birth.

"If you should have more children," she said, "they'll likely come fast with an even shorter labor. Some women were just made to have babies, and you're one of them."

I took three months off for maternity leave. While still on leave, I received a phone call from WLBT General Manager Dan Modisett.

The big boss.

"I want to talk to you about moving up to the chief meteorologist position," he said.

***

Long-time WLBT weatherman Woodie Assaf was in his eighties. His family was ready for him to retire and spend more time at home. Central Mississippians grew up watching Woodie give the weather every night. As nearly everybody knows,

Woodie always prefaced his forecast with *"The weatherman says..."* because he knew not to take credit for a forecast that didn't hit the mark—folks had been smiling about that for generations. He was a nice man and a true icon in the community, though.

And Dan wanted me to take his place?

Dan explained that Woodie would be retiring soon. Not only that, Walt Grayson, an equally nice man and a fine, veteran weatherman in his own right, wanted more time to focus on his "Look Around Mississippi" series.

Not only had WLBT never before had a chief meteorologist, Dan said, they'd certainly never had a female in that position. I was very aware that there were very few female chiefs at stations around the country. It was a tremendous opportunity, the answer to many, many prayers, and one of the biggest decisions I would make in my life.

It would seem to be a no-brainer, right?

Well, mostly. I sincerely enjoyed getting up in the middle of the night and co-anchoring the morning news. It was hardly a chore. I loved my morning co-workers, and my day was almost over by the time the day-shift folks got to work. Not only was I able to satisfy my interest in current events by having a hand reporting the news, but I was being used more and more in the weather department as a fill-in meteorologist. It was the best of all worlds in a lot of ways.

Truthfully, I was uneasy about replacing a legend. Woodie Assaf had given the weather on WLBT since the 1950s. I was thirty. Would viewers who'd watched Woodie for so many years give someone so young a chance?

And would they watch a woman give the weather, and take her seriously?

I was very honest with Dan about all of this. He assured me that everyone involved—most definitely Woodie Assaf and Walt Grayson—were solidly on board with the proposed change. I told Dan that having the blessings of those men was the *only* way I would even begin to consider leaving mornings and moving to nights.

Dan's reassurance and encouragement went a long way toward making me feel better. But I feared how it might play out in public: Would some of the loyal WLBT viewers think I'd somehow politically maneuvered my way into Woodie's job, forcing him into retirement and Walt Grayson to the sidelines along the way? I surely hadn't done that. But I had no control, of course, over reactions from viewers.

As I was on maternity leave when this discussion took place, Dan asked me to keep the offer private for the time being.

That was fine with me. It would give me time to pray and ask God what He wanted me to do.

***

Meantime, I was learning how to be a mother to Gracie and trying to get her on a sleeping schedule. I soaked in every single moment I had with her. I was, by most standards, an older mother, and I was ready for this newfound challenge. Moving to nights at WLBT would give me more time with Gracie, as I wouldn't have to go to work until early afternoon. If weather conditions permitted, I would even be able to go home for a couple of hours between the six o'clock and ten o'clock newscasts for supper—we call that a "dinner break."

When I returned to the morning newscasts after my maternity leave was up, I jumped back into the cycle of waking up before the crows fairly easily because being up for midnight feedings kept my body clock intact. Dan called me into his office that week and asked if I had considered the chief meteorologist offer. By then, after weeks of prayer and considering all the angles of the new position, I was ready to step out on faith.

I told him I'd be honored to do it.

***

Our marketing team created a series of weather promos spotlighting me as the new chief meteorologist and leader of the weather department. Given that I was also a part of the prime-time anchor team viewers watched each night, there were photo shoots with news anchors Howard Ballou and Maggie Wade and sports director Rob Jay. With my pals Wilson Stribling, Jack Hobbs, and Paul Williams at my side, I said goodbye to our morning viewers and began my stint on December 1, 2003, as the first chief meteorologist in the storied history of WLBT.

Gosh, what a thrill.

That's not to say that every single minute was easy. I went from being hidden behind a news desk to being fully shown on the air. Yes, that's something we in the news business are acutely aware of. There were many more viewer comments once I began working nights, and that was to be expected. Although the WLBT morning show has a vast audience, a *ton* of people watch their evening newscasts. Most of the emails and voice messages were encouraging. Some fit into the category of those I read and discuss at speaking engagements, and they continue to draw a lot of laughs from the audience. Most days I can roll my eyes and grin. The TV biz is not for the faint of heart, though, and if something gets under my skin, I try to shake it off and get back to work. Again, the great majority of comments—even in those first months after I replaced Woodie Assaf—were very positive.

Here's one I wasn't prepared for.

I spoke at a local church one Sunday morning. Afterward, an elderly gentleman walked up and introduced himself.

"I was in the barber shop the other day," he said. "Someone said you make all the decisions up there at WLBT and that you got Woodie Assaf kicked off the air."

I laughed, but he didn't crack a smile. He was quite serious.

I assured him that I didn't—and don't—have anywhere near that kind of power. Nor can I make it rain or snow.

I became more and more comfortable in front of large groups, especially when it came to sharing my faith. I could see God's hand at work in moving me into a television station with so many viewers. It gave me a chance to have a greater influence on those who had been going through trials in their own lives.

More importantly, I was able to share the importance of forgiveness. My two years at WAPT did not end like I'd hoped. But I was able to forgive. If it weren't for forgiveness, would God have moved me to WLBT? Would I have been listening to Him as He laid out a whole series of good opportunities in my year off the air? And would I appreciate WLBT as much as I do if that year off the air hadn't taken place?

***

Philippians 3:13 says, "…But one thing I do: Forgetting what is behind and straining toward what is ahead." Notice you can't move forward in life if you're looking behind you.

Colossians 3:13 says, "Bear with each other and forgive whatever grievances you may have against one another. Forgive as the Lord forgave you."

The Bible makes it clear: forgiving others is a command.

So many times, we don't forgive someone because we don't *feel* like it—it's easier to stay angry and upset. But God's Word doesn't tell us to go forward in life on feelings. It tells us to forgive others. End of story.

Mark 11:25 says, "And when you stand praying, if you hold anything against anyone, forgive him, so that your Father in Heaven may forgive you of your sins." This scripture says, *"If you hold anything against anyone, forgive him."* The Bible doesn't say, "Wait until the other person who has wronged you, spoken ill toward you, or defamed you, comes to you and apologizes before you forgive him." In today's society, that's what most people seem to think. But the Bible says that if *you* have unforgiveness toward someone, *you* forgive that person.

When I think about someone who had to exhibit forgiveness, I think about Joseph. His brothers sold him into slavery because they were jealous of him. Joseph went through some horrible years during that time, including serving time in prison. He asked his cellmates to remember him when they came before the king, hoping they would somehow mention Joseph's name and get him a reprieve from the king. It wasn't until Joseph was able to interpret the king's dream that he was let out of prison.

The king was so impressed with Joseph that he made him an empirical ruler. Then, years later, Joseph came in contact with his brothers—the very flesh and blood who sold him into slavery.

A massive famine had swept across the land, and his brothers came before him to beg for food. Joseph had a decision to make.

He could forgive his brothers for what they had done to him years before and grant them food from the storehouses. Or he could pay them back with death.

Genesis 45:8 tells us what Joseph did. He told his brothers, "So then, it was not you who sent me here, but God. He made me father to Pharaoh, lord of his entire household and ruler over all of Egypt."

Joseph realized forgiveness was not about his brothers—this was about him and his capacity to forgive. Joseph knew that in order to move forward in life, he had to forgive what his brothers had done. And because of the forgiveness Joseph showed them, he was able to save his whole family by providing them with food through the famine. Imagine what would have happened if Joseph had chosen the alternative.

The Third Key: Forgiveness is not an option. It is a command.

Although my heart ached at being off the air for a year, I had to forgive—the enforcement of the non-compete in my contract was a business decision. Looking back, I firmly believe God would not have moved me to WLBT if I'd chosen not to forgive.

God sure can't bless us if we have unforgiveness lying around.

The Fourth Key

Forecasts and Faith
Five Keys to Weathering the Storms of Life

The Fourth Key: Don't go through your storm without asking God to bless you.

I had been WLBT's chief meteorologist for just over a year when we found out we were going to have another baby. I had gotten pregnant so easily the first time, and the second time seemed just as quick. This baby would be due on June 12, 2005, which meant Gracie would be just shy of two years old. I had always wanted my children to be close in age because there were so many years between my siblings and me. My memories of them as a child are few, and I wanted my children to have many stories to tell of their days growing up. In return, hopefully, they would grow up together as friends.

Although some were very surprised I was having another baby so soon after having Gracie, I didn't see it as a negative. Dr. Travelstead even suggested I have my children before my risk of complicated pregnancies, pointing out that the risk of birth defects really increases after thirty-five.

This pregnancy started like my first. I was sick as a dog. The morning sickness lasted all day. I had pregnancy fatigue to go along with the nausea and vomiting, too. Before Gracie came along, I could nap whenever I wanted. Not now, though—not with a year-old baby toddling around the house and getting into everything. Sleep when she sleeps, I was told.

That was easier said than done.

William and I heard the heartbeat on my first trip to see Dr. Travelstead and were very excited. The sonogram showed a round mass of tissue with a strong, thumping heart rhythm. At six weeks along, I shared the good news with Dennis Smith, my news director at WLBT. My flat stomach had begun to swell so much faster than it did with Gracie. My clothes weren't fitting and were too snug around the waist. And that, of course, led to a few emails and voicemails from viewers.

From the moment I saw the baby on the sonogram, I felt "it" was a "she." It was too early to tell at six weeks, but this was a mother's intuition. Just as I had asked the Lord to lead me to a scripture to pray over Gracie when I was carrying her, I asked Him to guide me to a passage to claim for this baby. The Holy Spirit led me to Ephesians 3:17-19: "I pray that you, being rooted and established in love, may have power, together with all the saints, to grasp how wide and long and high and deep is the love of Christ, and to know this love that surpasses knowledge—that you may be filled to the measure of all the fullness of God."

At eight weeks, I announced to the WLBT viewing audience and my co-workers that I would be taking maternity leave for the second time in the summer of 2005.

***

After waking up every morning feeling as though I had a stomach virus, something was different when I awoke one morning in late November 2004. I felt as if I could run a marathon, and, goodness, this was a pleasant surprise! *Hopefully this pregnancy is going to be different after all,* I thought. *Maybe that elusive "first trimester sickness" was indeed true.* I welcomed the thought of coasting through the second and third trimester nausea free. When people asked me how I was feeling, I could be honest with them this time around and answer, "I feel great." And I did.

I went to Dr. Travelstead two weeks later for another checkup. This was part of the routine, the monthly checkup every mother has during a pregnancy. It had become quite obvious I was *with child* again. I looked like I had a cantaloupe hidden underneath my shirt, and I was just entering my fourth month.

As usual, I made small talk with the nurse in the exam room. She pulled out the Doppler device used to detect a fetal heartbeat. I lifted my shirt and waited for the messy goo to be rubbed on my stomach. She rolled the wand all around to distribute the jelly, and we waited for the swishing noise to come. She rolled the wand to my lower tummy.

Nothing.

"Hmm," she said with a puzzled look on her face. "Sounds like this baby is hiding. Let's try again."

I asked if that was normal.

"Yes," she reassured me. "Sometimes these babies like to move around and find another spot to get comfortable in." She continued to search for the next minute, but the heartbeat couldn't be found. "You know what, to keep you from sitting here any longer and letting me roll around on your belly," she said, "let's go do a sonogram. I bet we'll find it there."

Gracie's heartbeat had come up every time. This had never happened before.

***

The nurse escorted me to the sonogram room and told me to undress. The sonogram technician came in and greeted me warmly.

"So, this baby is trying to hide from us, huh?" she said. "Let's see what we can find."

She began her exam. I waited patiently, silently praying. *Come on, baby girl. God, let her find this child's heartbeat, please.* There, her form came into view. No longer was she a mass of unrecognizable tissue. This time, I saw her side profile with a perfect nose, two tiny hands and arms, and two skinny legs. But something was wrong.

She wasn't moving. She was just…there.

I scanned the sonogram technician's face for some sort of answer. Her expression was like that of a stone. She poked around on my belly, and the baby moved slightly in the amniotic fluid. Then she turned up the volume to the sonogram machine.

Nothing.

There was no sound coming from the sonogram machine because there was no heartbeat.

Our baby was dead.

The tech looked at me with sympathy written all over her face and told me she was sorry. Almost as if I didn't believe what I had just seen with my own eyes, I asked, "Sorry for what?" Deep down, there was a part of me that wanted to believe she was talking about something totally different than what we were there to do.

"The baby has no heartbeat," she said.

My heart felt as though it were coming up through my throat. The tech told me that there was Kleenex on the counter. Then she said she would leave me alone to get dressed before taking me back to Dr. Travelstead.

She closed the door. There I sat, all alone. What had just

happened? This was to be a routine exam. I'd told William there was no need for him to be there with me because I had done plenty of these checkups before. I knew he was busy at work and didn't want him losing an hour of his workday sitting in a waiting room, watching the clock tick away. But now, I needed him more than ever, and he wasn't there.

I wanted to scream to God, "Stop, so I can get off this ride *now*. Go find someone else to sit in this seat, okay?"

But it doesn't work like that.

***

I sat down with Dr. Travelstead a few minutes later. She knew I was stricken with a deep sadness, for she had been through a miscarriage herself. It was as if time stood still. I knew she had other patients waiting for her, but she acted as if I were the only one who mattered. She did all of the talking while I broke down and sobbed on her shoulder.

I had so many questions. How did this happen? I thought I was having another healthy pregnancy. Did I do something wrong? Could I have caused the death of our baby? Dr. Travelstead assured me that I did nothing wrong. She said it was probably a chromosomal heart defect that caused the baby to stop developing.

The worst part was yet to come. This was a Friday, and Dr. Travelstead wasn't available for surgery until Monday.

This meant I would have to carry the baby through the weekend, pregnant belly and all, and know my baby was dead. Just the thought of it made me cringe.

Dr. Travelstead insisted that her nurse take me out of the clinic a back way so no one would see my red, swollen eyes and tear-stained face. She knew I wasn't ready to be seen and wanted to make sure my privacy in that awful moment was protected. It was very, very kind of her.

I got in the car and pulled out my cell phone to dial William. "The baby's dead," I told him as I cried in the parking lot. William promptly said that he was on his way home. I called Dennis Smith from the car to let him know I wouldn't be coming to work that afternoon and why. He sounded as crushed as I felt and told me to let him know when I was ready to come back—what a wonderfully supportive boss.

Then I made the truly tough call.

I reached Momma at work. She answered in her typical jovial voice, and my voice was already cracking when I spoke. She knew something was wrong right away. Her voice began to shake as well when I broke the horrible news. She said that she would call Daddy, and they would come right away.

William arrived home and came straight to me. He put his arms around me and held me for what seemed like hours while I wept quietly on his shoulder. There was nothing for either of us to say, or perhaps we didn't *know* what to say. Sometimes just being next to the one you love is the only comfort at that moment.

I couldn't eat for two days. All I could think about was our little girl, lying inside me, dead. I slipped into a deep, dark depression. I had been upset before, but this was a place I'd never been. I didn't know anyone who had had this experience. This wasn't a topic people just brought up in everyday conversation. My first pregnancy was so easy and so predictable. What made this one different? And how would I explain that I might *look* pregnant, but I'm not anymore?

All I did was sleep and cry. Each time the phone rang, I let it go straight to voicemail.

My co-workers and close friends called to check on me, but I didn't want to talk to them. Florists made deliveries to the house, but I didn't answer the door. I didn't want to continue with this life.

***

Monday morning arrived. I didn't know what to expect with this surgery. The sadness I felt weighed a thousand pounds. I had planned how my next hospital stay would be when I delivered this child. But this time, the delivery wouldn't produce a healthy baby.

After an hour, I woke up in a fog.

"Mrs. Bassett?" the recovery room nurse called out. "Your procedure is over with. You did just fine."

My *procedure*? Why was this delivery being called a procedure? This was my baby, not a *procedure*.

***

I was wheeled out of the hospital and through the front doors to wait for William to pull my car into the pickup line. I heard people whisper as the nurse pushed me through the waiting area, *"There's Barbie Bassett."* Of all the times to be seen, I thought. I slipped into a deep depression—deeper than I've ever known before. Not only had I not brought home a baby, but my hormones were on a rollercoaster. My body—as well as my emotions—had to recover.

I took long drives and thought again and again about everything that had just happened to me. I wanted to mourn. I wanted to die. I wondered what would happen if I just drove off one day and never returned.

I contemplated how I wanted to die.

Overdosing? Slashing my wrists? Driving into water? No, that seemed like a long, miserable death. I wanted to end this misery as quickly as possible. I knew where my husband kept his gun. Pulling the trigger, if done right the first time, would be a painless, quick finish.

I gazed at my precious Gracie. She was learning how

William, Gracie, and me in November 2004.
I was pregnant with the baby I lost.

to maneuver at walking, running, and discovering everything around her. Would she make it without me if I checked out of this life? I shuddered when I thought about her growing into an adolescent—then into a young woman—with her whole life before her. And I would miss all of it.

William walked on eggshells around me. He was afraid of saying something that might trip my trigger and send me into a crying rage. I'm not quite sure he knew the extent of the desperation and thoughts of finality going through my head. Despite it all, he loved me firmly and purposefully.

***

It wasn't that I wanted people to miss me. But I wanted to disappear, and I didn't know how to verbalize my feelings. If I were to share my thoughts and my emotions with someone, they would suggest counseling. *I'm not crazy,* I kept telling myself. *I'm just sad.* I knew my church was praying for me and so was my family. I felt every prayer. I just didn't understand why God had allowed this to happen, knowing how this baby was so anticipated and already loved. I didn't feel like praising God through this personal storm, but I knew there had to be a much greater purpose for this heartbreak.

God was working on a testimony for me. I just didn't see it yet.

A week after losing the baby, I walked into a local store

and grabbed a shopping cart. As I made my way down an aisle, a mother and daughter caught my attention. I saw a young girl who looked about nine years old. She was hobbling toward her mother and looked as if she had polio or some type of muscle degeneration. Her legs were crooked, and she used a walker. Her mother called out to her, "Come on. We need to get some cereal."

I'm not one to stare, but I was mesmerized by this girl. I found myself thinking, *that could've been my daughter.* My eyes welled with tears, and I left the shopping cart in the middle of the store and got into my car. I laid my head on the steering wheel and cried.

I would've loved her just the same, God, even if she had a birth defect. So why did You take my baby away? I could've handled it. Here I had been praying for this baby and claiming the scripture that You led me to, God. And look what happened. I prayed for this child to know how wide and how deep and how high is Your love and now...this.

My heart was ripped apart. I was angry.

***

But suddenly I felt like Paul on the road to Damascus. The eyes of my heart were opened at once and I thought about the verse from Ephesians 3:17-19, which says, "...that you, being rooted and established in love, may have power, together with all of the saints, to grasp how wide and long and high and deep is the love of Christ." The sweet voice of the Lord was telling me the scripture had been fulfilled for our baby. She now knows how wide and how deep and how high is the love of God, because she is right there with Him.

Oh, wow.

I was realizing at that moment our baby was in the warm, loving arms of the Father. And that gave me an unspeakable joy. Talk about a rollercoaster of emotions.

I returned to work and felt I owed the viewers an explanation as to my whereabouts. It was obvious something had happened, as I wasn't sporting a pregnant belly anymore—there was no getting around that. So, while on the air with my co-workers Maggie Wade, Howard Ballou, and Rob Jay, I announced that I'd lost the baby and would appreciate the thoughts and prayers of the viewers. When I got off the air, I was flooded with emails and phone calls from people who wanted to share their miscarriage stories with me. Their support helped me more than they could ever know. I knew I wasn't alone anymore.

The tears became fewer although my heart still ached.

Dr. Travelstead suggested we wait a couple of months to give my hormones some time to readjust.

Three months later, we were pregnant again.

***

This time around, I was much more guarded.

I didn't want to talk about my news for fear of people asking more questions, as well as the fact that I was trying not to get my own hopes up. Once again, this pregnancy was starting out normally, although I was having some bleeding. The never-ending nausea was back, but I had never spotted before. I was afraid this pregnancy would end like the previous one.

Dr. Travelstead watched me like a hawk. I had an initial sonogram that showed the egg sac but no heartbeat yet. I was five weeks pregnant, and the heart had not started beating. We waited another week and prayed this little one's heart would kick in. The following week, I went back in for a sonogram, and there it was—thump, thump, thumping away on the sonogram.

I breathed a great big sigh of relief.

Knowing this baby was alive and well so far, I continued with my daily routine. At eight weeks, I announced to my co-workers that I would be going home for Christmas because this baby was due on Christmas Day. It was special already.

***

William went out of town on business in early August. I'd arrived from work and was getting ready for bed. When I took off my suit and put on my pajamas, I noticed blood. I was by myself—Gracie was asleep in bed—and I panicked. I called William and cried, "I think I'm losing the baby." He tried his best to calm me down and suggested I call Dr. Travelstead first thing the next morning. I did and was told to come in for a sonogram.

Right there on the screen was that little heart...still beating.

What a relief.

The sonogram tech explained that some women have bleeding at various times through their pregnancy. While I took it very seriously, of course, it wasn't always a sign of danger.

Just something we would continue to watch.

As I had done before, I asked God to lead me to a scripture passage to pray and lay claim to this child. The Lord led me to Zephaniah 3:17: "The Lord your God is with you, He is mighty to save. He will take great delight in you, He will quiet you with His love, He will rejoice over you with singing." Every morning, I would recite that verse over our son.

This time, we were having a boy.

***

The annual hurricane season is from June 1 to November 30, with the peak of activity in August and September. Anyone who lives along any coastline keeps an eye on the weather each summer and fall. Predicting how many hurricanes might develop—and certainly their direction and intensity—is one of the most difficult things for any meteorologist. The highly qualified team at the National Hurricane Center makes the best predictions they can. But as we all know, weather is hardly an exact science.

So by mid-August the peak of the 2005 hurricane season was just about at hand. All meteorological eyes were on the Atlantic and the twelfth tropical depression of the season. It had already been quite an active season. Hurricane Cindy had reached the shores of Louisiana as a minimal storm, Hurricane Dennis hit the Florida panhandle in July, and other tropical storms had threatened the Gulf.

A new disturbance formed over the southeastern Bahamas on August 23 and was quickly upgraded to tropical storm status the following morning. This tropical storm was given the name *Katrina*. The storm continued to move toward south Florida and was upgraded to a Category-1 hurricane just a few hours before making landfall between Hallandale Beach and Aventura, Florida, on August 25.

As storms cross land, they have a tendency to weaken. Hurricane Katrina did just that...initially. But one hour after emerging into the Gulf of Mexico, she was a force to be reckoned with. Katrina quickly intensified to a Category-3 hurricane.

Katrina was moving into unusually warm waters. During the summer, water temps in the Gulf can exceed 80 degrees Fahrenheit. The Gulf becomes a breeding ground for tropical development, meaning that the warm water gives hurricanes exactly what they need in order to sustain power. So not only was the storm intensifying, but the wind speed was increasing, too.

That spelled big trouble.

William and I were referred to in a *Clarion-Ledger* feature in July 2005 as a "crisis couple," meaning whenever there's a natural disaster in our area, both of us are affected. William is on the road doing medical evacuations while I'm forecasting the weather for WLBT. But when we had Gracie, things changed. We had to decide how to care for her in the event both of us were tied down with job responsibilities.

The week of August 23 was when we put our family plan into action. We made arrangements for William's parents, who live in Neshoba County, to take care of Gracie. Given that the Philadelphia area is well inland from the Mississippi Gulf Coast, we both felt confident leaving her with them for several days.

***

William prepared to head south. At that time, it wasn't clear where Katrina would make landfall. Whether she hit the southeastern coastline or not, chances were high William would be deployed to help organize and facilitate evacuations of hospitals and nursing homes. For me, it was looking as though I would be working long hours over the weekend.

But there was great disparity among the computer models on a pinpointed landfall location. What we in meteorology call "spaghetti plots" from the various hurricane models had Katrina making landfall as far west as the Texas coastline…to as far east as the Apalachicola, Florida, bay area…to every other location in between.

By the morning of Friday, August 26, Katrina had strengthened to a Category-3 hurricane in the Gulf of Mexico. By then, computer models were showing a targeted landfall near the Florida panhandle. But something just didn't seem right with that prediction to me.

That afternoon at WLBT, my news director Dennis Smith and I talked about where Katrina might come ashore and his plans for his news team in covering the storm.

"I just don't see this storm hitting the panhandle," I said. "I believe Katrina is coming straight for our coast."

"But all the other guys are showing a Florida panhandle landfall," he replied.

"I know they are," I said. "But I just don't believe that's going to be the case. Trust me."

What is female meteorological intuition? Well, I'd correctly forecasted my share of snowfall events for the Tennessee River Valley and a handful of snow events over the Magnolia State. In 2004, Hurricane Charley made landfall over Cuba with all projections moving him into the Gulf of Mexico. I had seen these storms make a last-minute curve several times before and had stated on my weathercasts that I believed Mississippi would be spared from Charley. Sure enough, Mississippi breathed a collective sigh of relief when Charley curved east and moved over south Florida as a Category-4 hurricane on August 13 of that year.

Just over a month later, Hurricane Ivan made landfall over southeast Alabama, moved northeastward along the Delmarva Peninsula, headed over south Florida, and emerged back into the Gulf of Mexico as a tropical storm. Most projections had Ivan possibly hitting the Mississippi Gulf Coast, but I continued to see Ivan make his westerly curve. As expected, Ivan made landfall over Cameron, Louisiana, on September 23. What an off-the-wall track.

These last-minute changes in direction dramatically impacted the landfall of the storms. Yes, nature has a mind of its own when it comes to weather events. But after having correctly forecasted a few major hurricanes and snowfall events, I felt more confident in relying on my meteorological and female intuition.

Around 4:30 that afternoon, my intuition was proving accurate. The National Hurricane Center noted that Katrina had yet to make the turn toward Florida and revised their official forecast.

They now included Mississippi as a possible landfall

location.

I ran to find Dennis again.

"We need to lead with weather," I said. "Katrina is coming straight for us."

"Are you sure? Everybody else is still predicting a Florida landfall."

"I'm telling you, Katrina is coming to the Pass Christian or Biloxi area."

***

Maggie Wade and Bert Case opened our five o'clock newscast with word of a change in the hurricane projection and tossed it to me. As I stood there in front of the green chroma key wall, I reminded the WLBT viewers of what I had alluded to earlier in the week.

"You need to make preparations *now* for this hurricane to reach the Mississippi Gulf Coast," I said, as I showed the estimated time of arrival. "Katrina looks to make landfall late Sunday night or possibly Monday morning." I went on to suggest viewers stock up on batteries, bottled water, generators, non-perishable foods, and have some cash on hand.

On the morning of Saturday, August 27, I checked the latest computer models to see if anything had changed. Katrina was still an upper-end Category-3 hurricane. The National Hurricane Center issued a hurricane watch at ten o'clock for southeastern portions of Louisiana, Mississippi, and Alabama. Things were getting worse.

I drove to the store to heed my own advice and make preparations for myself. With Gracie gone and taken care of, I only needed to concern myself with what I would need over the next few days. I withdrew money from the bank, picked up canned goods, snack bars, and bread, and made sure the car was gassed up. While I was in the store, a viewer came up to me and looked in my shopping cart.

"Looks like you're getting ready for a hurricane, Miss Barbie," she said. "I thought Katrina was going to Florida."

"Well, I said last night it was coming to Mississippi."

"Yeah, but I didn't really think it would happen."

I didn't really think it would happen.

That, tragically, was the mindset of so many people along our beautiful Gulf Coast and, I'm sure, the mindset of people who live on coastlines all over our great country. There will always be people who attempt to "ride out" major hurricanes. Maybe that stems from people not being physically able to see a storm like Katrina or Camille until it's right on top of them. Seeing that multi-colored mass on a weather map we meteorologists went on and on about just didn't make an impression.

But I, as a meteorologist as well as a wife and mother— a pregnant mother at that—knew that wherever this monster of a storm came ashore, there would be massive destruction. Katrina was going through an eye-wall replacement cycle, meaning it was collapsing on itself but continuing to grow. The storm had now doubled in size.

***

On the morning of Sunday, August 28, William and I said our goodbyes. I told him repeatedly how much I loved him, and he said the same thing to me.

"I don't have any idea when I'll be back," he said, rubbing my pregnant belly. "But I'll be thinking about you the whole time."

We had been through major storms before and were separated for a day or two, but we didn't know when we would see each other again this time around. He would be located in Gulfport at his paramedic headquarters.

The sheer size of Katrina by then was mind boggling. Her cloud canopy on the satellite images reached as far north as northern Mississippi and as far south as the Yucatan Peninsula. From tip to tail, this storm was like nothing many of us had ever seen before.

It was now a Category-5 hurricane.

Dennis Smith put the WLBT emergency weather procedure in place. I drove to work Sunday afternoon with toiletries and a change of clothes in hand. I spent the afternoon and early evening trying to decipher the latest computer models and calculations. I continued to stress to our viewers what type of storm we were dealing with. The phones were ringing off the hook—by then, many were beginning to realize the impact Katrina could have on their families and homes.

Maggie Wade arrived shortly after I did. Management put both of us at the news desk that evening, and we updated our viewers on various preparations and the opening of area shelters. At one point, I grabbed the latest forecast coming from the National Weather Service.

"Maggie," I said, "I need to read this to you and all of our viewers. This comes from the National Weather Service in Slidell, Louisiana." I took a deep breath and read the papers in front of me. "Hurricane Katrina, a most powerful hurricane with unprecedented strength, is rivaling the intensity of Hurricane Camille of 1969. Most of the area will be uninhabitable for weeks, perhaps longer.

"At least one half of well-constructed homes will have roof and wall failure. All gabled roofs will fail, leaving those homes severely damaged or destroyed. The majority of industrial buildings will become non-functional. Partial to complete wall and roof failure is expected. All wood-framed, low-rising apartment buildings will be destroyed. Concrete-block, low-rise apartments will sustain major damage, including some wall and roof failure. High-rise office and apartment buildings will sway dangerously, a few to the point of total collapse. All windows will blow out."

I took a second to steady myself.

"Airborne debris will be widespread and may include heavy items such as household appliances and even light vehicles. Sport utility vehicles and light trucks will be moved. The blown debris will create additional destruction. Persons, pets, and livestock exposed to the winds will face certain death if struck. Power outages will last for weeks, as most power poles will be down and transformers destroyed. Water shortages will make human suffering incredible by modern standards.

"The vast majority of native trees will be snapped or uprooted. Only the heartiest will remain standing, and those will be totally defoliated. Few crops will remain. Livestock left exposed to the winds will be killed.

"Once tropical storm and hurricane force winds begin, do not venture outside."

***

Later that evening, WLBT sent news crews to area shelters to show the number of evacuees who were arriving in central Mississippi. These people were tired, hungry, and confused. Some had been evacuated in previous storms, and they wondered if this evacuation was necessary.

More and more WLBT staffers came to work very early on the morning of Monday, August 29. It was quite literally an "all-hands-on-deck" situation at the station. Producers stayed on phones lining up interviews while photographers and reporters were sent to various parts of the state to cover the mass evacuations. Directors were shouting cues to those of us on the news set.

The storm coverage was mentally taking a toll on me. Physically, it was hard to keep my energy up. Not only was I five months pregnant, but standing for long periods of time was

Taking a break from Katrina coverage at WLBT while expecting Will

causing pain. My legs felt as though they were being punctured with tiny needles when I walked to the chroma key wall and back, or made similar trips to the weather lab. Maggie pointed out at one point that my ankles were swollen. Soon my feet swelled to the point they no longer fit in my shoes.

I continued to give updated Katrina coordinates through the long night, and our anchor team did the same thing. Video came in from the Louisiana Superdome, showing us images of the elderly, the poor, young children, and those with debilitating medical conditions. We would see them again and again in the days to come.

***

William called me one last time before daybreak.

"I miss you," he said. "How are you feeling?"

"Not so good, but I'm hanging in there."

He asked for my professional opinion on Katrina's latest storm track. Then he said there would come a time—most likely very soon—that we probably wouldn't be able to talk to each other.

"If these trees start snapping and the cell towers go out," he said, "you may not hear from me for a while. I just wanted you to know I love you, and that I'll talk to you whenever we establish communication again."

***

On Monday, August 29, at 6:10 a.m., Hurricane Katrina made landfall as a strong Category-3 hurricane near Buras-Triumph, Louisiana, with maximum sustained winds of 125 miles per hour. Katrina also made a third landfall in St. Bernard and St. Tammany parishes in south Louisiana as a Category-3 hurricane. We waited for video and any kind of information we could get so we could pass it along to our viewers.

Around eight o'clock, I heard from a friend who had family in the New Orleans area.

"My parents said water is rushing into the lower ninth ward, near the industrial canal," she said. "The levees have broken."

I dropped the phone and headed straight for the newsroom to tell the news producers. It was the first report we'd had of the levee breach.

By ten o'clock, Pearlington, Mississippi, was getting pounded. That landfall put the Mississippi Gulf Coast in the right front quadrant—the worst possible place to be in a hurricane because it was the area that would receive the highest storm surge, wind damage, and water damage.

That's exactly where my husband was.

***

Once Katrina made landfall, the storm went from being a weather story to a news story—a major news story that dominated our news coverage for a solid week. It was time to start covering the aftermath and continue the forecast for the high winds and heavy rain as the still-powerful storm plowed through central Mississippi like nothing people in our viewing area had seen in years, if ever. I worked throughout the morning and the rest of the day with little down time.

As many across south and central Mississippi lost their electricity with each passing hour due to the sustained winds of 40 miles per hour, WLBT continued to broadcast. The station never lost power although many businesses and restaurants just blocks away lost power once the winds picked up. That was fortunate because WLBT didn't have a generator at the time.

And our viewers, of course, were eager for information. If they weren't able to pick up the WLBT signal on their battery powered television sets, they heard our broadcasts on local radio stations that simulcast our news feed. Not knowing who was watching us as opposed to who was listening, we had to make sure we described every piece of video to the viewer or, in this case, the listener.

***

The baby growing inside me, meanwhile, seemed to be turning flips in my stomach. At times, it felt as though he was rolling from one side to the other. I lay on Dennis' couch and watched my stomach jump and my skin stretch. As Katrina roared farther inland, the barometric pressure dropped even further. My blood pressure was increasing, the swelling was getting worse, and I was having contractions.

I tried not to show my discomfort on television.

"Areas south of Interstate 20 are experiencing wind gusts over 50 miles an hour now," I warned on the air. "Folks, if you don't have to be out on the roads, please don't venture out. Just stay home and we'll be right here with you."

I was getting more concerned with every contraction. I knew low pressure areas could have adverse effects on pregnant women, but I had never been in this position before. I was worried about William's safety, the safety of my baby, and getting the pertinent information out to the public about Katrina.

We all waited and watched as the winds picked up speed. By early afternoon, there were sustained winds of 48 miles an hour with some reports of gusts that exceeded 55. Ambulances, because of their top-heavy frames, were temporarily shut down, as were tractor-trailers.

I called my mother-in-law to check on Gracie.

"We lost power a while ago," Sudie Kay Bassett said. "But we have the generator going. Gracie and I are eating the popsicles before they all melt."

I knew Gracie was in good hands and couldn't care less what her mommy and daddy were doing at the moment. She could eat all the popsicles she wanted, as far as I was concerned.

I was just glad she was safe.

***

Reports of power outages, downed trees, and damage came in to our newsroom. When I took breaks, I closed the office door. *Dear Lord, please make this baby settle down,* I thought to myself during one of those breaks on Dennis' couch. I'd hoped that being still and quiet would make the contractions stop. They would subside when I was still, but fire up again when I got up and walked to the news set to continue the weather updates. By then, our full weather team of Paul Williams and weekend meteorologist Eric Law was in place, and my opportunities to rest were more frequent as we shared the duties.

***

But something struck me while watching the news footage we were getting from the area shelters. Pregnant women, some looking like they were ready to deliver, were walking into the Mississippi Coliseum and other designated shelters with their families. I began to wonder about their conditions. I knew how the drop in barometric pressure and stress of the storm was affecting me, both physically and mentally, but I didn't have to leave my home. These women had to leave without the promise of being able to go back. My mind flashed back to the F-4 tornado in my neighborhood and the lives that were changed forever by the force of nature. To see the faces of those women shuffling into their temporary shelter homes made a deep impression on me, one I carry to this day.

There has got *to be a blessing in all of this mess, God.*

***

Genesis tells us the story of Jacob. You may remember that Jacob and his brother Esau were rivals from the very beginning. Jacob misled his father, Issac, and had him will the birthright to him, when in fact Esau was the firstborn. Esau was furious, and his anger put Jacob on the run.

Time passed, and the boys grew older and wiser. Jacob had grown spiritually and wanted to see his brother Esau and ask for forgiveness. He wanted to give Esau the blessing he deserved. He gathered his wives, his two maidservants, and his eleven sons and sent them ahead of him as they were preparing to meet Esau. Genesis 32:24 says, "So Jacob was left alone, and a man wrestled with him till daybreak."

Jacob was a strapping man and very strong. Although the Bible calls the wrestler a *man*, the story seems to indicate the man was a supernatural being in order for him to wrestle all night without tiring. But we learn later in Genesis 32:30 that the man was truly God in the flesh. In Genesis 32:25, we learn that, when the supernatural stranger saw he could not overpower Jacob, he simply touched the socket of Jacob's hip "so that his hip was wrenched as he wrestled with the man."

In Genesis 32:26, it says, "Then the man said, 'Let me go, for it is daybreak.' But Jacob replied, 'I will not let you go unless you bless me.'" The stranger didn't answer but instead told Jacob his name was no longer Jacob…it was now Israel. The Bible says God blessed Jacob right there on the spot, and Jacob named the spot where he wrestled Peniel. In Genesis 32:30, Jacob said, "It is because I saw God face to face, and yet my life was spared."

Jacob knew he had received mercy and blessing, and he now wanted the assurance that, somehow, he would overcome his brother's wrath. Also, God changed Jacob's name. Changing a person's name in those ancient times was a rite of passage that marked a significant change in that person's life. Jacob's name no longer meant *deceiver.* As Israel, it now meant *struggles with God.*

The Fourth Key: Don't go through your storm without asking God to bless you.

Even through the dark times, God wants to bless you. But you have to *ask* for that blessing. We get so caught up in our circumstances and doldrums that the last thing we often think about is asking God for a blessing. Jacob was not going to let God get away without asking for one.

The Fifth Key

Forecasts and Faith
Five Keys to Weathering the Storms of Life

The Fifth Key: Through the storms of life, speak your faith out loud.

Hurricane Katrina had slammed Louisiana and the Mississippi Gulf Coast. Recovery teams and volunteers were now trying to help storm victims locate missing loved ones and salvage any belongings that weren't destroyed or lost. The storm had moved over central Mississippi and people were stunned at what they woke to on the morning of Tuesday, August 30, 2005, which was a brilliant, sunny day.

Our WLBT photographers and reporters were doing their best to cover all angles of the story and stay atop the aftermath of the storm. Calls were coming into the newsroom from viewers looking for loved ones on the Gulf Coast. Communication towers had been damaged and land lines were down. Electricity was a scarce commodity, and we were being told some locations would go weeks without power. With lines down, the threat of electrocution still loomed. People were spending the night in parked cars, waiting for gasoline to flow again at local gas stations. Law enforcement agencies were asking residents to stay off the roads unless absolutely necessary until power lines and debris could be cleared away.

On the news set, our anchors were still broadcasting non-stop and giving contact information for the various relief agencies. The storm was over, but people were hungry for any information we could give them. Phone numbers were given to viewers, as we asked them to let us know if they had a missing relative they'd not heard from since before the storm.

I'll never forget the way we all huddled in the WLBT newsroom to see the aerial coast video shot by our photographer Joe Root in Skycopter-3, which was piloted by Coyt Bailey. These were the first pictures of Katrina that any Jackson TV station would have. Coyt narrated the video, showing the former locations of famous landmarks, casinos, antebellum homes, and condos.

"This is where the Treasure Bay Casino used to be," he said with the whipping of the chopper blades in the background. "The big pirate ship we always recognized from miles away is obliterated."

I quietly took in the washed-out road beds, flattened homes, and leafless trees. I thought of William and wondered if he was okay, as it had been two days since we'd spoken. *I don't know what that is…that looks like the Imperial Casino…there's an ambulance parked on the road! Is that William?* I just wanted to know he was alive. The suspense was eating away at me, and the lingering contractions and fatigue were more than I could bear.

I walked down the hall and back to my office. I closed the door and buried my head in my hands. All sorts of "what ifs" ran through my mind. *What if William can't call me to let me know he's okay? What if I go into labor and lose our son? What if William never comes home?*

***

William's secretary called the next morning.

"He's fine," she said. "All of our people are fine. He wanted me to let you know he's doing well and is being taken care of. He'll call you once he gets a signal or can get his hands on a satellite phone."

I can't put into words what a relief that call was.

As soon as I got off the phone, I answered one of the ringing newsroom lines. It was an evacuee who was nine months pregnant.

"I'm due any day, and I don't know which hospital I need to go to around here," she said hysterically. Not only was she unfamiliar with the hospitals in Jackson, she told me, but chances were high her doctor wouldn't be delivering her baby. "They tell me my house is gone and I have nothing."

I didn't know her, but I made a promise to help her. She and I had one thing in common: We were both pregnant. However dire my situation was, I knew where I would deliver, I knew how to contact my doctor when I needed to, and I had a warm bed to sleep on at night. This woman had none of that. The footage of the pregnant women and families walking into the shelters played over and over in my mind like a film clip that was stuck in an old movie projector.

Inspiration struck in that moment.

I felt the Holy Spirit compel me to organize a baby shower for the evacuees. But this wouldn't be just any baby shower.

It needed to be the city of Jackson's biggest baby shower.

I contacted the Agricultural Museum a few days later and asked if they would donate a large room where I could host the shower. A friend of mine contacted someone who made cakes and made arrangements to have a sheet cake donated that could feed 100 people. I called every hospital in the area and asked for representatives to set up booths to inform the moms-to-be about their facilities and the doctors who practiced with them. During my weathercasts, I asked viewers to donate items like diapers, baby clothes, strollers, high chairs, baby beds, and blankets. Two weeks later, I hosted what we decided to call Jackson's Biggest

Baby Shower with a few close friends who volunteered for the day and helped me put it together.

Deputies with the Hinds County sheriff's office kept order outside the shower and asked for identification. Although it was a free shower, our goal was to help pregnant women (or brand-new moms) who had been adversely affected by the powerful hurricane. We had to turn a few people away, like one woman who told a deputy she had several kids and had lost everything in her freezer. I brought her to the entrance of the vast room. Expectant mothers milled around the wooden floor speaking with hospital representatives in booths. Another set of pregnant women were in a corner picking out baby furniture that had been donated by a church.

"If you can honestly say that you're in need of baby items or furniture," I said with a gesture at everyone inside, "then you're more than welcome to join us. But these women have lost a lot more than what was in their freezer."

She turned around and walked out. I didn't see her again.

***

By the end of the day we'd served 88 women, including two who were expecting twins. Each was given a laundry basket with diapers, wipes, baby clothes, burp cloths, blankets, bottles, and formula. Those who'd lost everything were given baby furniture. All left with information about area doctors and hospitals.

Meanwhile, William got his hands on a satellite phone and reached me. I kept him updated on the pregnancy, how Gracie was doing (she would remain with my in-laws until the following weekend) and how things were going in the Jackson area.

Katrina taught me that in doing for others, I can find my heart's desire. The month after Katrina hit (September 2005) was a very difficult time, but the giving hands of others made it one of the most special times in our state's history.

***

One night in December of that year, I went home between newscasts to prepare dinner. William didn't look well and said he thought he was coming down with a stomach virus. When I arrived after the late newscast, he met me at the door. His face was stark white.

"I don't feel any better," he said. "I'm going to the emergency room."

He insisted I stay home with Gracie, who'd been asleep for several hours. I felt the urge to pray hard as the hours passed. I still hadn't heard from William by midnight. I was nine months pregnant, and we had already discovered our baby boy was in breech position and growing larger by the week. Breathing was uncomfortable and there was such pressure on my organs and diaphragm that I wasn't sleeping well under normal conditions.

I drifted in and out of sleep as the baby rolled in my abdomen. Then the phone startled me awake.

"Mrs. Bassett?" a voice said. "This is Dr. Copeland. I'm with your husband in the emergency room."

That brought me fully awake.

"Your husband has a perforated colon," the doctor said. "This is causing his bowels to leak, which can be fatal. We're going to have to remove a portion of his colon."

Dr. Copeland was about to operate—right then. He told me they couldn't afford to wait until I reached the hospital. I was too upset to cry when I got off the phone. I had gone through Hurricane Katrina not knowing William's fate, and now this. I got down on my knees.

Lord Jesus, You know I can't handle this right now. The doctor can't wait on me to get there so You are going to have to be there for William. Please give the doctor and nursing staff wisdom to see what they need to see and to fix William's colon. I'm not strong enough to take care of a sick husband and a newborn at the same time. And I'm most certainly not strong enough to be a widow.

***

Dr. Copeland called two hours later.

"Your husband is in recovery. I had to remove almost a foot of his colon and put a colostomy bag on him," he said. "His colon needs to heal, and then we'll reverse the colostomy in a few months."

I went to the hospital later that morning and found William in a deep sleep. Machines were beeping all around him, and he was hooked up to an oxygen supply while sleeping off the anesthesia. His color was gray. I had never seen my quiet, unassuming husband in such a vulnerable position. But William began acting like his old self after three days in the hospital. He was put on a lifting restriction for a specified time and learned how to change the colostomy bag on his own.

I knew we'd be back at the same hospital very soon, with that little baby boy kicking around inside me.

***

On the afternoon of December 14, I walked into the weather lab prepared to work like any other day. I felt a weird sensation and went right to the restroom—it seems my water had broken. I called Dr. Travelstead and asked her what to do.

"Come on in," she said. "I'll let the E.R. know you're coming. Whatever you do, don't push. Remember, the baby is breech."

It felt as though someone had a knife in my back. My contractions were coming every fifteen minutes, and I knew I had to get right to the hospital. I stuck my head in Dennis Smith's office and told him he'd better arrange for someone else to do the weather that night—I sure wouldn't be around. I drove myself to the hospital and called William to let him know what was going on. A security guard opened my car door when I reached the front of the hospital.

"Is it time, Mrs. Bassett?" he asked.

"It's time. Let's do this."

William Christian Bassett was born an hour later. Will was named after his daddy, and also after a song my mother used to sing when I was a child called, "I'll Tell the World That I'm a Christian."

***

My three months of maternity leave were spent learning how to adjust to two children instead of one. Will was such a blessing. After the loss of our baby girl, the rocky start to this pregnancy, and the stress of Katrina, I hadn't felt I could enjoy the last nine months. But when I held Will in my arms, there was a sweetness I came to adore.

I was a bit torn about returning to work. I wanted to enjoy every minute with Gracie and Will, yet I knew I had such a tremendous responsibility of being a public servant in forecasting the weather. The week I returned from maternity leave, I received some nice mail from viewers welcoming me back to WLBT. Most said they had missed me and were glad to have me back in my old spot again.

Much to my surprise, William was brought in to cut my hair
for Pantene's Beautiful Lengths Donation Day.

A few calls and emails weren't quite as supportive.

"Are you still pregnant?"

"I thought you just had a kid. How many more kids are you gonna have, anyway?"

For every viewer comment that hurt, there were supportive ones from women who'd been where I was—women who knew how hard it was to be a working mother and away from her children.

***

One morning while feeding Will and watching *The Today Show,* I saw a new hair donation program for cancer survivors called Beautiful Lengths. The Pantene hair care company had just announced it on *The Today Show* with the inaugural cutting of Hollywood actress Diane Lane's hair. Beautiful Lengths makes wigs from hair donations, which are given free of charge to women who've lost their hair to cancer. After watching the segment, I looked at my own hair in the mirror and wondered if I could donate it.

I called Momma to find out if anyone in our family had been diagnosed with breast cancer in the past. We hadn't, thankfully. Then I read a staggering statistic. According to the American Cancer Society, 85 percent of new breast cancer cases every year are diagnosed in women with no prior family history of the disease.

That could be me, I thought. *I don't have a family history.*

***

I went to a visitation a few weeks later for Dennis Smith's sister. She'd died of breast cancer. As I walked past her casket to pay my respects, I noticed she lay in the casket bald. I was moved beyond words. No, I couldn't fight anyone else's cancer, but I could sure donate my hair for women who were fighting for their lives.

One day Stephanie Bell Flynt and I got on the subject of hair while chatting. Mine had grown full and thick from the pre-natal vitamins I took while expecting Will, and I told her I was going to grow it very long and have it cut for Pantene's Beautiful Lengths.

Stephanie said she'd do it with me.

We set out on a campaign to educate the public on the need for hair donations. What began with two ladies talking about hair woes turned into almost 900 people donating their hair at the Mississippi Institute for Aesthetics, Nails, and Cosmetology. We wound up making *The Guinness Book of World Records* for the most hair donated to a charity in a 24-hour period.

We were awestruck by the sheer number of women, men, and children who joined us to give the gift of hair. The donors came from all socio-economic backgrounds and had their own stories. Some were breast cancer survivors and knew what it was like to lose their locks. Some had family members who'd lost their battle with cancer. But many of them had not been affected by cancer—they just wanted to give. They couldn't afford to donate money for cancer research, they told us, but they could donate hair to someone they might not ever know. Our hearts were warmed by the faces we met.

Thanks to all those donations, a wig bank was set up at St. Dominic Hospital in Jackson where cancer survivors can now go pick out their own wig and walk out without paying a dime.

Stephanie Bell Flynt and me, with our donated hair

Stephanie and I even involved our daughters the following year. I was always explaining to Gracie why I had to cut our playtime short because I had a volunteer meeting to attend. Just as my parents had done with me, I wanted to teach her at an early age what giving was all about. I knew that involving her in the hair-growing process would teach her the importance of sacrificing for others. So with the help of Stephanie and her daughter Stevie, Gracie and I donated our hair together the following year.

***

Tragedy struck again on July 12, 2007, when my older brother Doug, the hardest-working farmer I've ever seen and only 47 years old at the time, suffered a major heart attack. When Momma called me early that morning with the news, William and I jumped in the car and raced to the hospital in Oxford to be with my parents and Doug's family. We were overwhelmed by the number of people who were in the waiting room to support my family and who told us they were praying for him.

During one of the five-minute visits we were allowed to make to the intensive care unit every few hours, we were led to the partitioned room where Doug was hooked up to a myriad of machines. Tubes were coming out of every hole in his body, and a pump was working his heart for him. The doctors gave us the grim news. Doug's heart had suffered massive damage, and the outlook wasn't good. The only thing we could do was pray.

I walked over to the nurse's desk and asked the nurse on duty if we could gather some people to pray over Doug. She asked how many people I was talking about, and for some reason I settled on ten. I think I found a kindred spirit in the nurse, because she gave me permission. Ten of our friends and family members held hands and encircled Doug's bed. We didn't know how much, if anything, he could hear. But the Holy Spirit showed up in that moment. A calm, warm, peaceful feeling came over all of us as we lifted Doug heavenward.

Later, my parents and I saw a young woman standing over her aging mother. We struck up a conversation with her, as she had been sitting in the waiting room with many of us.

"Did I hear y'all praying in there?" she asked with a tear in her eye. "Would you mind coming in here and praying for my mother?"

The elderly woman was suffering from complications of diabetes. We prayed for her, too.

***

Doug slowly began to improve. Doctors implanted a cardiac defibrillator in him, and he was released after two weeks in the hospital. Momma said something interesting happened to him on the way to the hospital, though.

"He saw The Light," she said.

Tony Womble, the helicopter pilot in charge as Doug was flown to Oxford, told us that he heard Doug talking to the flight medic one minute, and then he heard the medic yelling, *"Clear!"* several times as he shocked my brother the way doctors have to do to start someone's heart beating again.

This was a story I had to hear for myself.

I wanted to wait until he'd had some time to recover before I put on my old reporter's hat and began asking questions, though. I went home to visit with him and my parents in August. Doug spent an hour telling us what he remembered and answering our questions. The last thing he remembered while in the ambulance helicopter was hearing the pilot say, "Six minutes out," meaning that they were six minutes from the hospital in Oxford.

Everything went black at that point.

Then Doug said he was in a peaceful place with whitish/gray matter surrounding him—resembling clouds—and that he saw a bright light ahead.

"It was ten times brighter than the sun and illuminated everything with the most beautiful, purest color of light," he said.

Although Doug said he was walking straight toward The Light, he could not feel anything touching his feet, nor did he look down at his legs. He just had the sensation of walking. I asked if he was floating.

"No, I was walking," he said. "The temperature was

perfect. That sticks out in my mind."

He said he knew exactly who *The Light* was, and that he felt drawn to it. Doug said the first person he kept telling himself he wanted to see was our maternal grandfather. He was such an instrumental leader in our family and was always giving spiritual insight.

"Did you think you had died?" I asked him. "I mean, did you think about us down here? Did you think about your family?"

He gave me a surprising answer.

"No, I had no knowledge that I had died. I didn't think about anybody here on earth. I was in a perfect state of peace."

***

In our society, we are led to believe that those who've gone before us are aware of what we're doing here on earth. But Doug's experience was much to the contrary. It gave me great consolation in knowing our baby girl wasn't in Heaven looking for me or her daddy. Instead, she was busy praising the Lord and, no doubt, at the feet of many of the saints who'd gone before her.

Doug said the next thing he knew, the stretcher was shaking as the paramedics were taking him out of the helicopter.

"Then I saw a doctor looking over me," he said. "He asked if I knew who I was."

Doug said although he was dead for only a short while,

it felt as though he spent hours in Heaven. We also talked about a family member for whom we've been praying, and how burdened our heart was for this family member to come to Christ.

"I was on my way to Heaven, and I want to go back," Doug said with a tear in his eye. "I want to make sure everyone knows it is real."

***

The Wiggs' 50th anniversary photo, complete with all the grandkids

I love the message in Philippians 3:20: "our citizenship is in Heaven." Yes, we have an earthly residence. As Christians, though, we have an address in Heaven, too. Knowing my brother has an address in Heaven is such a blessing.

After spending a few days with my parents and Doug, William and I learned we would be adding another member to the family. This was quite a surprise to both William and me. As with my other children, I asked God to direct me to a specific scripture I could pray for this child. He led me to Ephesians 1:16-17, which says, "I have not stopped giving thanks for you, remembering you in my prayers. I keep asking that the God of our Lord Jesus Christ, the glorious Father, may give you the Spirit of wisdom and revelation, so that you may know Him better."

This new Bassett would be due in the early spring. I had grown accustomed to the nausea since it seemed so common with the others. Dr. Travelstead watched me closely again, every step of the way. Sadly, William's mother, Sudie Kay, passed away early in the pregnancy. Her death brought a lot of sadness during that period, as she loved her grandchildren with everything she had and was such a special woman.

In the wee hours of April 3, 2008, we drove to the hospital for a scheduled cesarean section. The guard welcomed us at the back gate, and I was wheeled upstairs to the hospital room. A few hours later, Lillian Faith Bassett was placed in my arms. She was named after another one of my favorite hymns, "Have Faith in God."

Raising children in this day and age isn't easy. There are certainly more distractions to vie for their time and attention. Mix in a career, speaking engagements, homeschooling, and being a wife, and my life doesn't get any easier—only more complicated. Juggling so many balls at once isn't as easy as a clown makes it look. But ask any good juggler, and he will tell you that the key to keeping all the balls in the air is focus. Keep your eyes centered on the ball in front of you, and all the other balls will follow suit.

In that same way, Christ is my center. I wouldn't be able to maneuver all of the tasks at hand were it not for the solid faith I have in Jesus Christ and the hope I carry in my heart every minute of every day, knowing who I am *in Christ*.

II Corinthians 5:17 says it best: "Therefore, if anyone is in Christ, he is a new creation; the old has gone, the new has come." Knowing who I am in Christ has made me open and ready to see the glory of God.

***

One of my favorite people in the Bible to study is Abraham. This man had monumental faith, and he didn't think twice about speaking his faith.

You remember his story. Abraham and his wife, Sarah,

had wanted a son for years. They didn't think they would ever see the promise God made to them. They even took the matter into their own hands because they were running out of patience with God. After Abraham had fathered a child by Sarah's maidservant, Sarah finally conceived years later.

Many years later.

She was in her *nineties* when she found out she was expecting God's promise. The baby boy God promised was given the name Isaac. I don't doubt Isaac was a mama's boy and the apple of his daddy's eye. So imagine Abraham's astonishment when God told him to sacrifice Isaac. This was a test—a test straight from the hand of God. Genesis 22:2 says, "Go to the region of Moriah. Sacrifice him (Isaac) there as a burnt offering on one of the mountains I will tell you about."

Notice that God didn't tell Abraham which mountain to go to—He only gave him the region to which he was to travel. Abraham got ready for the journey and saddled up his donkey and prepared his two servants to make the trip with him and Isaac. Genesis 22:4 says, "On the third day, Abraham looked up and saw the place in the distance." Abraham had been traveling for three long days. Ever felt as if you were on a road to nowhere? You know God is prompting you to make a change. You feel in your spirit God has something else better for you. You have no doubt God is wanting you to put your trust in Him, but you seem to be traveling down a road with no end.

Genesis 22:5 says, "He (Abraham) said to his servants, 'Stay here with the donkey while I and the boy go over there. We will worship and then we will come back to you.'"

Abraham was speaking his faith. I don't believe Abraham was trying to be sly toward his servants. He wasn't lying to them. Abraham was speaking out loud what he believed God was going to do. He believed God was going to provide an animal for him to sacrifice instead of his son. Otherwise, Abraham would not have said, "*We* will come back to you."

The Fifth Key:
During the storms of life, speak your faith out loud.

The Bible clearly states Abraham's journey and the command to sacrifice his son was a test by God. So does God have to test us to find out what's in our hearts?

No, but tests of faith are not to enlighten God. Tests of faith are to teach us. When God tests me, it helps to uncover my real motive for doing something. Tests help to clarify my loyalty and to nurture genuine faith.

Summary

Forecasts and Faith
Five Keys to Weathering the Storms of Life

Summary

When you look back at all the keys, you'll see how they all

point to the cross. As with any key, it unlocks something. Keys

might look different, but they all have the same purpose. You will

also notice each key has an action to it. They just don't happen,

just as a key won't unlock a door without being in someone's

hand. They won't help you weather your particular storm if they

aren't put into practice.

The First Key: Trust God's plan for your life.

Romans 8:28 says, "And we know that in all things God
works for the good of those who love Him, who have been called
according to His purpose." God is working in *all* things: good,
bad, and everything else in between. This promise is *for those
who love Him*. Those who are in rebellion cannot depend on

achieving good in their lives. God desires to work in us in a spiritual, eternal way. This prepares us for future glory. Romans 5:3-5 says, "Not only so, but we also rejoice in our sufferings, because we know that suffering produces perseverance; perseverance, character; and character, hope. And hope does not disappoint us...."

Those who dwell on their storm or their suffering never gain His benefits or achieve a higher perspective. But those who focus on what God can do while going through their storm and suffering will be strengthened. God is allowing you to go through this storm for a reason He knows will manifest His glory in you. Trust His hand.

The Second Key: Praise the Lord, even when things aren't going your way.

Telling God how marvelous He is when our world seems to be falling apart makes no sense to the average person. The two just don't go together naturally. But praising God through the storms of life will put who He is into perspective. Psalm 9:10 says, "Those who know your name will trust in you, for you, Lord, have never forsaken those who seek you." When you praise the Almighty One, you are telling Him, "I trust you even though I don't understand."

Psalm 18:2-3 says, "The Lord is my rock, my fortress, and my deliverer; my God is my rock, in whom I take refuge. He is my shield and the horn of my salvation, my stronghold. I call to the Lord, who is worthy of praise, and I am saved from my enemies." God is solid as a rock, firm as a stone, and immovable. Our praises may come and go, but He never leaves us. That is worth praising Him for.

The Third Key: Forgiveness is not an option.
It is a command.

This key is the hardest for most people to comprehend, and there's good reason for it. Who would want to forgive someone who has done them wrong? But I believe that in forgiving others, we unleash strongholds that have been hovering over us for years. Think about the families who have unforgiveness for another family member. Perhaps you are one of them. Many people are angry at others, and have been for years, and don't even remember why they got angry at them in the first place!

Romans 4:7-8 says, "Blessed are they whose transgressions are forgiven, whose sins are covered. Blessed is the man whose sin the Lord will never count against him." When you are blessed, you are full of joy. You are content and happy. But to be blessed is more than a feeling. Being blessed is the result of having the right relationship with God. Having unforgiveness puts a strain on your relationship with God, just as it does in any relationship. If you are unforgiving of someone else, don't expect God's best to flow your way. You are deliberately hampering His goodness, prosperity, and victory from coming into your life.

Colossians 3:13 says, "Bear with each other and forgive whatever grievances you may have against one another. Forgive as the Lord forgave you." Because Jesus forgave you and died on a cruel cross for you, you can surely forgive others. It's not easy. It's not fun, and it will go against every feeling you've ever had. And notice God never says in His Word to "forgive, but only if you feel like it." It's not in there. You won't find it. Forgiveness is a command by God. Forgive others and you will change your family tree.

The Fourth Key: Don't go through your storm without asking God to bless you.

When bad storms come into our lives, we have a tendency to focus on the negative. We focus on how miserable our life is, and how we are barely making it through. Stop the insanity. You wouldn't go plop down thousands of dollars for a new car and walk off the car lot without it, would you? So why go through a personal trial without asking God to bless you through it?

II Corinthians 12:9 says, "But he said to me, 'My grace is sufficient for you, for my power is made perfect in weakness.' Therefore I will boast all the more gladly about my weaknesses, so that Christ's power may rest on me." The apostle Paul is saying here that God's favor and loving kindness and mercy prepare him for anything he could encounter. Paul wanted to make sure that in any weakness he had, God would bless him when He brought him through the storm.

Psalm 84:11 says, "For the Lord God is a sun and shield; the Lord bestows favor and honor; no good thing does He withhold from those whose walk is blameless." Someone who is blameless isn't someone who is perfect, but someone who has undivided loyalty. Being blameless in the Biblical sense is someone who seeks God's will. No one is completely blameless before the Lord since we have all sinned but, when God grants forgiveness, we become blameless in His sight. And when that happens, He doesn't withhold good from you.

Proverbs 10:22 says it best: "The blessing of the Lord brings wealth, and He adds no trouble to it." Through your storm, humbly ask God to bless you as you go through it and as you come out the other side.

The Fifth Key: Through the storms of life,
speak your faith out loud.

I know I am married to a most loving, compassionate, and giving man. When I speak to the man I believe my husband to be, the words reiterate the feelings in my heart. We have all read in the Bible the importance of memorizing scripture, and there's good reason for it. II Corinthians 10:4 says, "The weapons we fight with are not the weapons of the world. On the contrary, they have divine power to demolish strongholds." Most weapons we are familiar with are defensive, but the Word of God is offensive. It chases away the enemy.

Faith is active. It has a voice. We can release God's Word through our prayers, by confessing His Word out loud, and by taking God-inspired action. James 2:17 says, "Faith by itself, if not accompanied by action, is dead." Therefore, we are blessed in the *doing* part of faith, not just in the *knowing* of faith. Release your faith as you release the scriptures out of your mouth and get ready to see wonderful changes and blessings in your life. Instead of being a victim of your experiences, make your experiences a victim of you.

At the end of the day, you either believe that God will leave you swimming in the deep, all by yourself, or that God is sovereign and can lead you out of the storm with blessings on the other side.

3-17-12